TRUE GROWTH®

"This book is a beacon of hope for those
searching to live lives of authenticity. The life stories
and lessons shared are invaluable."

–David L. Cook, PhD, Sports Psychologist,
Author/Executive Producer, Seven Days in Utopia

SIMPLE INSIGHTS ON
HOW TO LIVE AND LEAD WITH
AUTHENTICITY

TRUE GROWTH

AN LWM III CONSULTING SOUTION

Copyright © 2017 by LWM III Consulting Published by

True Growth® Publishing
11141 Monmouth
San Antonio, Texas 78239

Book design by Bruce Gore | Gore Studio, Inc.
Nashville, TN

Library of Congress Cataloging-in-Publication Data is available

ISBN: 978-0-9993258-0-3
Printed in the United States of America

True Growth® and Seasons of Growth® are registered trademarks of
Byrd Baggett and LWM III Consulting LLC, respectively.

Acclaim for TRUE GROWTH

"We always built our football program on four pillars: Communication, Trust, Respect, and a Common Purpose. You will find these as a common theme in the many insightful messages from a lot of learned people which are contained in this work. It is a recurring theme of wisdom where the power of the mind opens us to all kinds of possibilities with a "can do" attitude of resolve and commitment."

—Mack Brown, ESPN/ABC College Football Commentator, Former Head Football Coach, University of Texas Longhorns

"Success in dealing with life's struggles begins with knowing oneself. The True Growth insights on authentic leadership presented in this book will afford readers with the opportunity to gain a better understanding of themselves and in so doing be better prepared for dealing with the challenges in both their work and personal lives".

—Len Fullenkamp, Colonel, U.S. Army, Retired, former Professor of Military History and Strategy at the Army War College

"True Growth is a wonderful, must-read book, one you will read and re-read, then share with friends and colleagues. Whether you lead a family, a multi-national corporation, or anything in between, True Growth is a book that will help you develop as a person and a leader. It's a book of stories—many very moving, all very real—that provide grist for reflecting on the kind of person and leader you are. Every reader will benefit from this book. I sure did."

> **—Lieutenant General Jim Dubik,** U.S. Army Retired, PhD, Senior Fellow, Institute for the Study of War, author, *Just War Reconsidered: Strategy, Ethics, and Theory.*

"True Growth is a must read, and should be on every authentic leader's list of books to encourage inspirational growth and 'from the heart' leadership."

> **—Michael Overholt,** Vice President, American Contractor's Insurance Group

"In this age of information overload, I loved the simplicity of this book. Every chapter was a thoughtful lesson and reminder of what it takes to be a successful leader. As the world moves so quickly around us, it is nice to be reminded that the small details are truly why we succeed."

> **—Tricia Cullop,** Head Women's Basketball Coach, University of Toledo

"Ever since I took the True Growth class, my world view changed dramatically. Your book not only helps me relive the class with your motivational true-life stories, the questions asked after each story are insightful and make you dig deep to find answers. The book recommendations are so appropriate to the theme you are emphasizing. I would recommend this book for all that wish to better themselves."

—Ken DeBruhl, Vice President, Roebbelen Contracting

"Living authentically is no easy feat. The True Growth Book shows us the path. The insights and stories remind you that you don't have to live the story to learn from it."

—Felicia Allen, Principal, Felicia Hall Allen and Associates, former NIKE Manager of Women's Basketball and Team Executive for the WNBA Charlotte Sting

"The stories and lessons I have learned from the True Growth Leaders are truly everlasting. If you took each lesson in this book and replaced it with a stone you would end up with a solid foundation to live your life by; a life full of spiritual, emotional, personal and business successes. I hope you enjoy these lessons as much as I did and still do."

—Mike Moran, President, Cajun Industries LLC

CONTENTS

FOREWORD

Based on my experiences as a senior leader over many years, in different circumstances, this book is an invaluable resource. Each of the 15 distinguished authors, all members of the True Growth team, provide unique insights based on real events or experiences. In its own way, each chapter causes the reader to think about how authenticity and caring make better leaders. While I would encourage those interested in developing their approaches to leadership to participate in the True Growth Program as a student, all will not be able to attend. For them, this book provides the collective wisdom and experiences of some of America's truly eminent leaders. I firmly believe it will serve well to enhance the reader's understanding of how to become a more effective leader as well as a more fulfilled person.

After spending almost 30 years as an Infantry officer in the United States Army, I spent another 20 years as a career civil servant, consultant, and presidential appointee in the field of emergency management. Over these years I developed some definite ideas about leadership, especially leadership in crisis. Some of these views grew during my two deployments to the Republic of Vietnam and many other Army assignments. Others I learned during my service as Federal Coordinating Officer (FCO) (senior on scene representative of the Administration during presidentially declared disasters). One of the most memorable experiences as FCO was with Governor Haley Barbour during the response to Hurricane Katrina in Mississippi. The time I spent as FEMA's Operations Section Chief at the World Trade Center (WTC) certainly provided me lessons in humility and compassion, and a look at senior leaders' actions in a crisis.

During my four years in Washington as FEMA's Director, Disaster Operations, particularly during Hurricane Sandy, I witnessed good, and not so good, leadership at the strategic level. I learned there are clearly principles of leadership that are the same whether one is in battle dress or wearing the DC uniform, (a dark suit, white shirt, and conservative tie).

Over those almost three decades as an Army officer, I was fortunate to have served with and worked for some outstanding leaders. Lieutenant General (Retired) Lawson W. Magruder, III was one of them. In this book, *True Growth: Simple Insights into How to Lead and Live with Authenticity*, Lawson, his friend and business partner Byrd Baggett and their co-contributors, some of America's most seasoned leaders, provide the reader with actual experiences and anecdotes, as well as guidelines. Each chapter provides insights on how challenging situations were encountered and dealt with, some successfully, some not. In each chapter, the author shares how the experience provided lessons learned for the future.

I first met then Lieutenant Colonel Magruder in 1986 when he was teaching at the Infantry School while I was attending the Pre-Command Course. It was later, when Colonel Magruder commanded the 2d Brigade, 25th Infantry Division (Light) that I experienced his outstanding leadership. I had been the commander of one of the battalions of the Brigade for over 18 of the 30 months I spent in command. The Brigade was sorely in need of a positive, inclusive leadership environment. Lawson's influence was immediate. The authenticity and enthusiasm he exuded was contagious. It came from a real caring for soldiers and their families, the development of junior leaders, as well as his tactical and operational expertise. That was 1989.

Twenty years later I agreed to come out of semi-retirement in Hawaii to join my friend Craig Fugate in Washington. He had been nominated by President Obama to serve as FEMA's Administrator. We had been together for the many months I served as FCO for the four major hurricanes that struck Florida in a six-week period in 2004. Joining the Administration, I was appointed to be the Associate Administrator, Response and Recovery, responsible for all of the operational elements of the Agency.

Besides my deep respect for Craig, the reason I left beautiful Oahu was that I had seen the morale of my former colleagues at FEMA (I had retired in 2005 after conditions were stabilized in Mississippi) plummet in the aftermath of the flooding in New Orleans as a result of Hurricane Katrina. Other impacts on FEMA's self-confidence had to do with the uncertainties and loss of identity associated with becoming one of the 22 "legacy agencies" that made up the newly formed Department of Homeland Security. Adding to the loss of what in the Army we called "espirit de corps", was the rapid expansion of the workforce. Following

Katrina, Congress, for the best of reasons, provided resources to FEMA for the rapid expansion of its numbers of personnel. Many of these had never served in an organization in which its members were subject to deployment at a moment's notice into disaster areas. These assignments often involved Spartan conditions, discomfort, and long hours of work. Significant numbers of the recent members of the FEMA team did not seem focused on the mission: providing assistance to Americans in need. They needed to be convinced that, as Craig stated, "every FEMA employee is an emergency manager".

Turning around the morale of some of the members of the FEMA team was one of our first priorities. From those years during which we rebuilt the Army after Vietnam, I firmly believed training would be a key component to the rebuilding effort and to operational success in the future. I was taught two important things about training: "train as you fight" and "train to doctrine". Unfortunately, FEMA had absolutely no operational doctrine. We quickly put together a team of very experienced folks and developed a body of documents that provided guidance on how FEMA, and its state and federal partners, should operate jointly in the field.

Another critical component to the rebuilding effort was something else I had learned years before. As the Army reinvented itself following Vietnam, it was faced with the need to develop effective leadership training. An entire series of leadership courses were developed or revised under the Non-commissioned Officers Education and Officer Education Systems. When we approached FEMA's Emergency Management Institute (EMI) in search of leadership development programs, we discovered almost all of EMI's courses were technical in nature.

None would meet our need to develop leaders.

It was about that time when my old boss, mentor, and friend, Lawson, came to visit me at FEMA Headquarters in Washington. While his visit was mostly to catch up on the events that had transpired for each of us over the years, he mentioned that he, along with Byrd Baggett, had founded The True Growth program. We discussed the approach. It focused on authenticity and enhancing personal worth. It sounded like a real possibility in terms of meeting the need for a program to assist us in developing our leaders at FEMA. We agreed that I would send a small contingent of "scouts" down to the program. I selected my most trusted and operationally experienced deputy to lead the team. He had been with me on almost every large-scale disaster and national special security event for 15 years and was now a member of the Senior Executive Service. As a former offensive center for a professional football team, he focused on moving the ball down the field. I had absolute confidence that he would return with a solid recommendation on whether or not True Growth was appropriate for our supervisors. His report was overwhelmingly positive. He believed True Growth would be an excellent fit for our supervisors. We wanted them to become leaders as well as managers.

Since we formed a partnership with True Growth in 2009, over 300 managers (GS 14 and 15, and members of the Senior Executive Service) attended the program. We sent a diverse group of folks, some former members of the military, some up and coming graduates of prestigious universities with little operational experience, and some more seasoned civil servants. The feedback, from even the most strident activist types, was overwhelmingly positive. For some, it was a life changing experience.

In conclusion, there were operational benefits to sending managers to the True Growth program. The largest disaster during my tenure in Washington was Hurricane Sandy. During that large-scale event, almost every one of the graduates of the program, at that time, held key leadership positions. We were proud of the manner in which they performed their responsibilities as leaders, whether they were in the field or running the National Response Coordination Center in Washington. We attributed much of FEMA's performance in preventing a very big disaster from becoming a national catastrophe to the leaders who were alumni of True Growth.

The assessment of the program's impact on FEMA by the recent Acting FEMA Administrator (the former "senior scout" back in 2009) is that, "True Growth's influence on our leadership team has been profound. Definitely changed the atmosphere in the Response Division and allowed people to move forward in their careers".

—William (Bill) L. Carwile, III
Colonel (Retired), US Army
Former Associate Administrator, Response and Recovery
Federal Emergency Management Agency

INTRODUCTION

THE SEED FOR THIS BOOK was planted in 2007 when we, as perfect strangers, met at the urging of our spouses Gloria and Jeanne for breakfast at a greasy spoon café north of San Antonio in the beautiful Hill Country of our native Texas. After a marathon four-hour breakfast, we left with a vision to create a leader development experience that would help people become more authentic and effective leaders at home and work. The inspiration for our model was the majestic Mystic Oak, a 300 year old oak tree growing on the banks of the Guadalupe River. It was only natural that we named our leader development experience, True Growth.

Even though we had big plans, we never dreamed that ten years later more than 10,000 leaders would have benefited from the True Growth experience! Since our humble beginning in 2007, our team of facilitators and coaches has grown from the two of us to 38 seasoned practitioners committed to helping leaders embrace the transformational power of authenticity to improve themselves and the lives they touch. This world-class team has truly been the key to our growth and success.

Back to the evolution of this book. As part of the True Growth experience, we developed a 360° assessment based on the 7 core competencies and corresponding 25 behaviors of an authentic leader. For the thousands of leaders who benefited from this assessment and their one-on-one coaching sessions, we decided to publish a free monthly newsletter that focused on these seven core competencies that are essential to becoming an authentic leader. Each of these newsletters was written by a member of our team with the goal of sharing a personal story that brought to life one of the competencies.

The response to the newsletters was overwhelmingly positive. Not only did the readers, True Growth Alumni, enjoy the impactful real-world stories, but they saw great benefit from the True Growth Takeaway, Reflection Questions, and Book Recommendation that were included with each newsletter. That information allowed them to go deeper into making that competency an integral part of their life.

This book is our way of sharing these True Growth lessons on how to become an authentic leader. It is organized into seven sections focused on the behavioral competencies of an authentic leader. We encourage you to read each chapter deliberately, focus on the True Growth Takeaway, and, most importantly, take time to reflect and act on the Reflection Questions included after each chapter. We have also included at the end of each section some specific behaviors you should consider using to improve as a leader at home and work.

Our hope is that this book serves you well on your journey to leadership authenticity!

—Lawson Magruder & Byrd Baggett

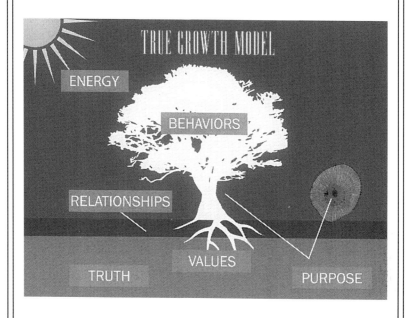

VIRTUES OF AUTHENTIC LEADERS:

- Authentic leaders have clarity of purpose.
- Authentic leaders are committed to living their core values.
- Authentic leaders are disciplined in their behaviors.
- Authentic leaders understand that truth is the lifeblood of growth.
- Authentic leaders understand that managing energy, not time, is the key to high performance and personal renewal.
- Authentic leaders understand that growing relationships is what really matters.

SECTION ONE

AUTHENTIC/HUMBLE

CHAPTER ONE

A Story of Authenticity, Courage and Hope

Lawson Magruder • *April 2015*

THIS MONTH MARKS the 40th anniversary of the end of the Vietnam War. It was a war that cost our great nation over 58,000 killed and 363,000 wounded. There has been much written and debated about the war "we lost" but I would like to devote this article to a friend, a brother who not only fought in the war but is from South Vietnam. It is a story of authenticity and hope and courage. The remarks below are from a speech I gave two years ago in San Jose, CA in honor of my friend, Nguyen Cong Luan.

Good afternoon everyone. It is a tremendous honor for my wife Gloria and me to be here at this book presentation for our dear friend Luan. We have known him for over 40 years and consider him a member of our family and a "brother".

If I may, I would like to spend my time speaking personally about Luan the friend, the soldier, and the family man. My comments are based upon personal observations, time with his family and months of reviewing and editing his book. If I get somewhat emotional, it is because Luan's story is one of

Calling, Character and Conduct of the most authentic leader I have ever known.

First, Luan our friend:

We first met Luan in July 1974 at Ft Benning Georgia when we attended a course for Infantry officers. I was a Captain who had served in Vietnam a few years before and was selected as the class leader. Luan was a Major, the senior allied student and Gloria and I were his class sponsors. Over the next nine months, we would forge a bond and friendship that would last a lifetime. Luan was not able to bring his family with him so he became a member of our family. He joined us for so many significant family events: welcoming our second child Loren into the world; playing with our oldest daughter Shannon to include a memorable trip to Disneyworld; sharing in our special holiday and family traditions; and participating in the many fun class parties and events. It was a remarkable year for our young family to have a "new member" of our family to enjoy time together.

Our lasting impressions of Luan during that special time together were: His zest for life and how he savored every moment of the day; his incredible sense of humor; his ability to forge personal friendships; his tremendous memory; and how much he always talked about his wife and children and how much he missed them.

Next, I would like to speak about Luan the soldier:

I watched Luan the soldier each day for nine months and I can unequivocally state he is the most authentic military leader I have ever met. We sat by each other every day and totally immersed ourselves as young leaders in learning more about military doctrine, tactics and techniques. I loved Luan's thirst for knowledge, his grasp for military history, his inquisitive mind, his creative thinking and his transparent nature. Needless to say, he understood counterinsurgency operations better than anyone in our class because he had observed it as a child and prosecuted it throughout his career as a soldier.

Of special note, Luan was extremely admired by all the leaders in our class which was represented by over 15 nations. Luan knew how to connect with leaders from very diverse backgrounds. As a result, our class was touted for years as "The International Class that got it right". Our Allied officers were greatly inspired by Luan's leadership. Personally, I learned a great deal from Luan about the Vietnam War- a war I had fought in as a young lieutenant from 1970-1971 in Quang Ngai Province. He broadened my perspective during an important period in my career and it served me well over 3 decades of service.

Last, I would like to talk about Luan the Husband, the Father, the Grandfather and the Brother:

As I mentioned, we started our course at Benning in July 1974. Of note, our class graduated in mid- March 1975. As the class was winding down, by late February, the North Vietnamese Army was starting its final invasion of the South. It was a sensitive and nervous time for the five South Vietnamese officers in our class. By early March, the situation in South Vietnam was very grave. Many felt the end was near. Luan and the other four were offered diplomatic asylum in the United Sates. I remember talking to Luan about this and without blinking an eye, he said he must go home to his family and fight for democracy to the end.

Gloria and I absolutely understood his decision was motivated by his love for his family and his Nation. The final two weeks were full of emotion as we spent time with our friend. It was a sad day when we bid Luan farewell after graduation. I thought we would never see him again but my beloved Gloria was ever hopeful and prayerful.

We departed the next day for a new assignment at Fort Lewis Washington and Luan departed for home. We last spoke on the phone on the 1st of April 1975 right before Luan got on a plane from Travis Air Force Base outside of San Francisco. By then the northern provinces of South Vietnam had fallen to the Communists. We told Luan how much we loved him and would be praying for his and his family's safety. We said our tearful goodbyes to our friend, our brother and then we hung up. Through my tears, I looked at Gloria and said: "Honey, we will probably never hear from him again".

Over the next month we watched the images and video coming out of South Vietnam and Saigon and realized the country had fallen. We prayed for the safety of our friend and his family. Gloria wrote letters for months but we never heard back from Luan and the letters were never returned.

Through the years, I am somewhat embarrassed to admit, I lost hope for my friend but Gloria never did. She always said, "We will see him again". I remained in the Army and over the next eleven years we moved many times.

In 1986, I was a Lieutenant Colonel and found myself back at Fort Benning, responsible for the same course that Luan and I attended a decade before. Over the next year, as I walked the halls of the Infantry School, many strong images of Luan and our time together 11 years before kept coming back to me.

Then one day I received one of the most important gifts in my life- a smuggled letter out of Ho Chi Minh City from our friend Luan!! There is no way to express the joy Gloria and I felt and the thanks we gave the Lord that night for delivering Luan back into our lives.

Over the last two decades we learned more about Luan and his family's journey to the United States. We have marveled at their courage while Luan spent seven grueling years in Communist reeducation camps. We have admired his son's journey to the United States as a boat person. We have been humbled by their love and devotion for one another, their assimilation into a new culture, their academic and professional achievements, and their patriotic zeal for their adopted Nation.

In closing, for those of you who have read his remarkable book, you know what Luan endured over the intervening years since we last saw him. His is the story like many of yours in the audience: one of remarkable courage, of love of family and of indomitable hope and Faith.

For those of you who have not read Luan's memoir, you are in for a tremendous journey when you read it. It is a book for the ages. A book written by a friend, a soldier and a family man; a book written by a victim who never lost his purpose in life during the darkest of times; a book written by a leader who was always true to his values and demonstrated impeccable character every step of the way; and it's a book written by a man who has conducted himself with highest integrity throughout his lifetime. I strongly encourage you of all generations to read Luan's book to get the complete picture and whole truth about the War in Vietnam.

Once again Ladies and Gentlemen, thank you so much for this opportunity to say a few words about our friend and brother Luan.

Lawson W. Magruder III—LTG US Army Retired—A Proud Vietnam Veteran

EPILOGUE: My final reunion with my friend, Nguyen Cong Luan, was his funeral January 25th, 2017 in San Jose, where he and his family, and many Vietnamese, settled after coming to the U.S. to live the American Dream.

True Growth Takeaway: When in your life have your personal values strengthened and sustained you during the most challenging times?

True Growth Reflection: Is there a decision you made because of a conflict of values? What did you do and would you do the same thing if you had a chance to do it again?

Recommended Reading: *A Nationalist in the Vietnam Wars: Memoirs of a Victim turned Soldier* by Nguyen Cong Luan

CHAPTER TWO

Not an Easy Thing to Do

Bob Dare • *November 2014*

Some years ago, although it seems like yesterday, I endured the ugliness of combat. The details are not important. Suffice it to say that I returned from Viet Nam, a 19 year old kid, angry, bitter, confused and disillusioned. Reintegration with society was more easily said than done. Although I legally could not drink, I had access to those who were and, as with many immature young people I drowned my emotions with alcohol. I was headed down a very dangerous path and was clueless as to how to reorient myself. Worse, I don't think I was even considering reorientation.

Then a day came while I was home on leave and my mother demanded that I meet her at work and take her to lunch. She scolded me severely and told me it was time that I realize that life goes forward, not in reverse.

What could I say, this was my mother and she was extremely persuasive. I cleaned myself up and showed up at her office, somewhat uncomfortable, but there just the same. Mom greeted me and began to introduce me to many of her co-workers. I was growing impatient, and as politely as possible suggested that we go eat.

"Just wait a minute, Mom said, "There is someone I want you to meet".

A few minutes passed and then, approaching from the back of the office building was a young woman who immediately caught my eye. This was the person Mom had wanted me to meet. The requirement for me to be brief here precludes me from filling in all the events that took place after that meeting but Karen became my girlfriend, then my fiancée, and ultimately, my wife.

But that is not the end of this story. Karen and I began dating and she immediately detected my attitude and she saw my growing habits of self-destruction. Why she didn't walk away from me is still a mystery but then again, God does work in mysterious ways. Karen became my friend. She did not pry for my internal thoughts and emotions. She listened and offered only silent consolation. She would wake me from my nightmares, listen to anything that I had to say and never tried to analyze me, but would always be encouraging in a positive manner. She would not tolerate my excessive drinking unlike so many others who had become enablers to my bad habit.

And so, the day finally came when Karen said to me, "The longer you hold the negative feelings inside the longer you will deny yourself the rest of your life."

With that warning, I began to open up to Karen. Not all at once, but slowly, and over time, I realized that letting go of the ugly past was medicine for the soul. It opened new doors to my life that I had kept closed. It made me realize that those internal wounds never heal as long as you keep them internal.

Needless to say, Karen's wisdom and careful but loving approach to helping me had everlasting effects and 43 years after saying "I do" she remains my best friend and confidant. No, I am not completely healed and doubt that I ever will be. But I obviously overcame the worse and reoriented myself to a path of productivity. For this I can thank my best friend.

True Growth Takeaway: Everyone needs someone that he or she can count on to be a true friend; someone who will listen without judging; someone who will enable you to work towards being your best. Are you a true friend? Do you have a true friend?

True Growth Reflection: Who are my real friends and why?

Recommended Reading: *Same Kind of Different as Me* by Ron Hall and Denver Moore

A dangerous, homeless drifter who grew up picking cotton in virtual slavery; an upscale art dealer accustomed to the world of Armani and Chanel; a gutsy woman with a stubborn dream. A story so incredible no novelist would dare dream it.

It begins outside a burning plantation hut in Louisiana . . . and an East Texas honky-tonk . . . and, without a doubt, in the heart of God. It unfolds in a Hollywood hacienda . . . an upscale New York gallery . . . a downtown dumpster . . . a Texas ranch.

Gritty with pain and betrayal and brutality, this true story also shines with an unexpected, life-changing love and friendship. If you only read one book this year, this should be the one!!

CHAPTER THREE

The Power of a Positive Attitude: "Don't worry. You'll find them."

ANNE MACDONALD • *November 2014*

IT IS OFTEN SAID that nothing good happens after midnight. That saying held true for me as a battalion commander. One dark February night at Fort Campbell I received a call from a flight crew at 0200 hours (2 a.m.). During night vision goggle (NVG) training, a set of aviation NVGs had accidentally fallen out of an aircraft. The U.S. aviator night vision systems were extremely expensive and highly sought after by both our friends and adversaries. In the wrong hands, the goggles could do serious harm to our technological advantage.

Missing, lost, gone, unaccounted for—whatever the word used—the lack of accountability of a high dollar item, triggered a series of events including immediate notification to the Brigade Commander, Division Commander and the XVIII Airborne Corps Emergency Operations Center. For our battalion, it meant standing down what we were doing and putting a 100% concentrated effort on recovering the goggles.

In the middle of the night there was no stand down. In fact, the task was the exact opposite—getting folks to stand up—to wake up and begin the search. Finding a set of night vision goggles, a device six inches by four inches in size, a set that had "accidentally fallen out of the aircraft somewhere over the Fort Campbell Reservation", would be a daunting task by any measure. The Fort Campbell Reservation covers over 100,000 square kilometers: the goggles could be anywhere.

I called my Battalion Command Sergeant Major and Executive Officer to prepare a search plan. As I got ready to leave our quarters, my husband "warmly" offered, "Don't worry. You'll find them!"

I thought, "Right. You who get to go back to sleep."

When I arrived at the battalion, a search party made up of the full flight company had been assembled. The young Soldiers, who obviously had been hastily awakened, had no idea why they were at the hangar this time in the morning. The 1SG was explaining to them how a set of aviation goggles had fallen out of the aircraft during night flight operations. Their task would be to find the goggles. As I looked at their dejected faces and the hopelessness in their eyes, I knew I had to say something.

Much to my surprise the first words I said were those of my husband's, "Don't worry. We will find them." (These words had stuck in my mind. They were a seed of hope.) I saw the Soldiers visibly square off their shoulders and stand a little taller. They got it. "Don't worry. We *will* find them."

The power of positive words! Those words put us into the right frame of mind. Science tells us that we perform significantly better when we are in a positive state of being. We had to start our search with an attitude that would at least attract a positive outcome. The last thing we needed was to quit before we even had started.

Fortunately, this story had a good outcome. We started our search at the last known place of accountability of the goggles—a huge landing zone located close to the airfield. Standing side by side, we began our sweep of the field. After hours of searching, walking shoulder to shoulder with only flashlights to guide us, we found the night vision goggles. What a glorious sound when we heard a soldier cry out, "Stop, I think I just hit something!" All flashlights went to the sound of his voice, then to his feet. And there on the frozen ground, amongst the stubble of cut hay, was the most beautiful site—a set of night vision goggles!

How many times do we look at a task and feel defeated or want to quit before we even start? A positive attitude can set the conditions to foster a positive outcome. A significant part of leadership is to swallow misgivings, paint a realistic picture of the desired outcome and with a positive mindset . . . "get 'er done."

True Growth Takeaway: Never underestimate the power of being positive!

True Growth Journal Questions: How has the power of a positive attitude changed the course of an event in your life?
Describe one positive thing that happened to you in the last 24 hours.

Recommended Reading: *The Power of Positive Thinking* by Dr. Norman Vincent Peale.

An all-time classic by one of the most inspirational individuals to grace the earth. If you've read it, read it again; if you haven't, it's a must read!

CHAPTER FOUR

Whose Plan Was This?

Bob Dare • *July 2014*

"OPEN AND HONEST communication is the lifeblood of healthy relationships."

Having spent 28 years in uniform I began to accept that my tenure as a soldier was close to ending. So, in 1996 I began to listen to offers that were coming my way. One afternoon at the Joint Readiness Training Center my cell phone rang.

"You don't know me", said the voice at the other end. "I got your name from a friend of mine in the Pentagon and would like to discuss a job with you. I know that you are not thinking about retirement but we are interested in what you might bring to our organization".

"I am open to hearing what you have to say", I responded. One thing led to another and before you knew it I had a written offer that seemed pretty fair and would allow me to leave the Army on my terms. I struggled with the decision for almost two weeks. I did not tell anyone of what I was considering.

Karen, my wife of then 25 years, knew that I had interviewed and that I had found the company interesting. She had no idea of how serious I was in taking the offer, that was, until 2:30 in the morning when I woke her and told her to go find a house on the other side of 285. "You're serious" she said.

"Yes, I am. I am going in and put in my paperwork this morning."

I did what I said I would do and the series of events that occur when one makes a life decision began unfolding. The house was bought. The retirement date was set. A ceremony was planned. It seemed as if 28 years had happened within a 24 hour period. All so fast, but all so exciting.

I retired on a Friday at 10 o'clock in the morning. The ceremony was memorable and many family members and friends made their way to Ft McPherson, Georgia to be part of a major milestone in my life. I retired in grand style and was sent off to start a new chapter in my life, grinning from ear to ear. The household had been relocated to the new residence and following the retirement festivities I closed the passenger door for Karen and drove north to 3904 Berwick Farm Drive, Duluth, Georgia. That weekend was consumed with setting up the new home, but my mind was on the new job and the excitement of my second career. The following Monday morning I was out of bed at 4:00 as usual. I ran my 3 miles, showered and put on my suit and tie and drove off to my new job.

A couple of weeks elapsed. One evening I came home to find Karen in a somewhat distraught mood. The house was rather messy. No dinner was planned, much less ready.

"Is there something wrong with you?" I asked. "Do you really want to know?" asked Karen "Of course I do!"

"Bob, for 25 years we were a team. Very few decisions were made that we had not discussed. We planned all of our moves together. We may not have agreed on everything but we always found a way to work things out for the best. Then, in making the biggest decision in our lives, you totally excluded me. We never discussed retirement. You woke me up and told me to go find a house. You had a ceremony, dropped me off here and went on your merry way. All you did was change uniform and an office. You left me behind at Ft McPherson. You dropped me here where I have no commonality with anyone. I feel like I was deserted and that you never considered anyone but yourself in this significant change of lifestyle."

I was taken aback and immediately realized that Karen was totally correct. I had lived in a "Season of Self" without regard to my partner, my friend, my wife and confidant. I had taken the "we", "us" and "our" out of our equation that had served us well over the course of our Army career. I had disregarded the personal sacrifices Karen had made to be an exceptional military spouse. I had taken her for granted that she would easily conform to what I saw as just another permanent change of station. What a selfish and thoughtless person I had been. I apologized profusely, begged forgiveness and spent hours discussing how to move forward.

This July marks 43 years for our marriage and partnership. It should go without saying that from that crater I created in 1996 to this date, communication between Karen and I have been very healthy.

Decisions are arrived at mutually and our relationship is sound. Oh yeah . . . and, I have not slipped back to a "Season of Self".

True Growth Takeaway: "WE" decisions are the key to healthy relationships.

True Growth Reflection: What one behavior do you need to change to be more of a "WE" listener?

Recommended Reading: *The Givers and the Takers* by Cris Evatt and Bruce Feld

The following endorsement speaks to the worth of this book: "Being a Giver is no better or worse, healthy or less healthy, than being a Taker. This book will help you recognize the manipulative potential in both personalities." —*The San Francisco Chronicle*. This book is chocked full of gems that, when applied, will help you develop deeper and more fulfilling personal and professional relationships.

CHAPTER FIVE

Gettysburg Lessons

BYRD BAGGETT • *May 2016*

"This is the last you may ever hear from me.
I have time to tell you that I died like a man.
Bear my loss as best you can.
Remember that I am true to my country
and my greatest regret at dying is that she is still not free
and that you and your sisters are robbed of my youth.
I hope this will reach you
and you must not regret that my body cannot be obtained.
It is a mere matter of form anyhow.
This letter is stained with my blood."

—*A dying Confederate Soldier's last words to his mother,
Friday, July 3rd, 1863*

WHEN I SAT DOWN to write this newsletter, I was reflecting on the impact of our True Growth Academy that we host in Gettysburg, PA. It's been less than a week since the May session, when our team and 28 client leaders gathered to explore the transformational power of authenticity. I still get emotional when I think of the ultimate sacrifice that was paid by eight thousand men at the Battle of Gettysburg. Of those casualties, more than 3,000 were Union Soldiers fighting for the rights and freedom of slaves as well as the unity of our Nation, and almost 5,000 were Confederate Soldiers fighting to sustain their way of life. Even though people will continue to debate which side was most honorable, no one will disagree that these men were committed to a cause greater than self. For me, a proud Texan, I am grateful for the way the Civil War ended, as the outcome preserved our country and is why we are blessed to be living in the United States of America.

We always end the True Growth experience on Thursday with a tour of the battlefield—the purpose of which is to study the various leaders and how they led, both successfully and unsuccessfully, during the three days of battle. Our guide for the day is Len Fullenkamp, an eminent expert on the Battle of Gettysburg. During the eight stops, Len brings to life the respective battle, insights into the lives of the key leaders and the impact that their leadership styles had on the outcome. Len does a masterful job of aligning his message to bring to reality the impact of both authentic and inauthentic leadership, as the purpose of the True Growth experience is to help our clients embrace the transformational power of authenticity to improve themselves and the lives they touch. After Len's narration, the 28 leaders break into groups with one of our coaches to discuss lessons learned from Len's analysis. Most importantly, our coaches encourage their group of 4-5 leaders to apply one of the lessons learned that will help them become more authentic in their leadership roles both at home and work. Following are the group's takeaways from the May 2016 True Growth Experience:

- Surprised as to the leadership relativity/lessons learned from the 'Battle' and how they apply today.

- Thoughtful, thought provoking, reflective opportunity to learn lessons on this battlefield, that not only help us to understand our nation and government but give us leadership lessons from them that apply to today. Also, personal appreciation of what my ancestors did for our country.

- Conceptually, it was a top down, bottom up way to look at leadership and apply it to our lives.

- Great focus on leadership.

- Everyone learns one's own life lessons from someone else or your own experiences. It was a great application of what we learned in class.

- The reality/importance of dealing with uncertainty.

- The realization that decisions have to be made even when you don't have 'all' the information needed.

- The importance for leaders to be flexible, willing to change plans/adapting.

- Surprised as to the leadership relativity/lessons learned from the 'Battle' and how they apply today.

- Leadership challenges don't always come when you're ready for them. Expect the unexpected.

- Not all leaders are the ones in charge. Subordinates are

leaders too and can make a difference at critical times.

- A leader has to know himself/herself and other leaders too if they, as a team, are going to achieve success.

- Small decisions make big waves (ripple effect). Said another way, "Tactical decisions can have strategic consequences."

- Leaders discussed the importance of being there for their people especially when confusion, rapid changing situations were occurring.

- We had some dialogue about delegating and motivating—how to transfer their passion and emotion.

The last stop on the battlefield tour is the cemetery where Abraham Lincoln gave his inspirational Gettysburg Address. When I reflect on the time we spent on that hallowed ground, words will never be enough to express my gratitude for the dead, wounded and missing American soldiers who, 153 years ago, willingly sacrificed their lives and futures for a cause greater than self. I, as one who never had the privilege of serving in the military, am so thankful for all the men and women who made the ultimate sacrifice to protect the freedoms that I too often take for granted. My hope and prayer is that we never forget the debt we owe these true heroes—their sacrifices saved our great Nation.

True Growth Takeaway: Never forget why America is "the land of the free and home of the brave."

True Growth Reflection: List three blessings of being an American.

Recommended Reading: *Killer Angels* by Michael Shaara —Winner of the Pulitzer Prize for Fiction in 1975. If you are going to read one book about the Battle of Gettysburg, this is the one! The following testimonial says it all . . .

"A book that changed my life . . . I had never visited Gettysburg, knew almost nothing about that battle before I read the book, but here it all came alive . . . I wept. No book, novel or nonfiction, had ever done that to me before." —Ken Burns, Filmmaker and Co-Author of *The Civil War*

TRUE GROWTH REFLECTION: AUTHENTIC/HUMBLE

Reflect on the following behaviors that are essential to being an Authentic and Humble leader:

- The leader is genuine and not trying to imitate someone else in speech, expressions or gestures. Viewed as the real deal and not modeling or emulating anyone else.
- The leader puts the interest of others and the team ahead of his/her own self interests.
- The leader avoids the limelight while ensuring team members receive recognition for their performance.

If you need to work on being a more Authentic and Humble leader, select the one behavior that needs the most attention and develop three actions that you will work on within the next 30-90 days to shore up this competency:

1. _____

_____

_____

2. _____

_____

_____

3. _____

_____

_____

SECTION TWO

TRANSPARENT

CHAPTER SIX

Giving Thanks

LAWSON MAGRUDER • *November 2016*

THANKSGIVING HAS BEEN my favorite holiday for as long as I can remember. Let me explain why.

Six of my Thanksgivings as a child were celebrated overseas as the son of a soldier. Whether it was in England, France or the Philippines, our family always gathered on that special day to eat turkey and a scrumptious meal prepared by our beloved Mom. In a foreign land we took time to give thanks for being blessed to have been born in the greatest democracy in the world. It was a time for us to express our love for one another and to pray for members of the Magruder and Windrow clans celebrating the holiday across a vast ocean in our beautiful country. As a young child and teenager and now as a husband and parent, I love the fact that Thanksgiving is focused on spending time as a family communicating our thanks to one another and not focused on unwrapping gifts or playing with new toys or trying on new clothes. It truly is about connecting with those we love so much.

As a soldier for over 32 years, Thanksgiving day was always

the most special day of the year for me. I think it truly started Thanksgiving Day of 1970 in the Central Highlands of Vietnam. That day was a transformative, healing day for me and my soldiers. In order to understand why, let me briefly tell you what preceded that special day.

On November 12th 1970, I was a 23 year old infantry officer leading a 28 man platoon. That day around 11:30 in the morning I had an entire squad—8 brave soldiers—killed by an enemy mine. In an instant, my platoon's world was rocked and our lives were changed forever. After a beautiful memorial service the next day, we were back into the treacherous mountains on another two week mission. It was the hardest leadership challenge of my life, as each of my soldiers and I sought out an invisible enemy while fighting back overwhelming emotions of anger and sadness. I also internally challenged the existence of my God and started questioning whether the loss of our brothers was worth it. However, over the next 14 days, I was able to put the sadness and pain and darkness on hold as we banded together and focused on the dangerous tasks at hand and welcoming new replacements into our outfit. Then on Thanksgiving day, light started coming back into my life but it took a while. We were moving out of the mountains that morning to get to low ground to pause and have a hot meal—a Thanksgiving meal—for the first time in two weeks. As we were navigating a challenging jungle trail, an explosion occurred and our hearts sunk. One of the most popular soldiers in the company was severely wounded. Our movement was delayed for 90 minutes as he was treated then evacuated by a medical helicopter.

Fortunately, he survived but sacrificed a limb that day for our Nation. Around noon we reached the low ground and went into a perimeter defense and then a helicopter arrived. Off hopped our Brigade commander with our First Sergeant and two cooks and several mermite containers with our Thanksgiving meal complete with turkey, dressing, mashed potatoes and all the trimmings. First Sergeant also brought the weekly mailbag with letters from home. I will always remember my soldiers' smiles and absolute gratitude for this pause in the action and our ability to taste and celebrate America for 90 minutes. After hearing an uplifting, inspirational message from our colonel after consuming a great meal and quietly pausing to read a positive, loving letter from my beautiful wife Gloria, hope and my God started to return to my life. Although the pain of that crucible in my life has never gone away, I will always be thankful for Thanksgiving day 1970 when the light and healing started in my life.

Another reason why I love Thanksgiving is because, in a military unit, it is the one day a year when the vast majority of the single soldiers are there for the holiday and will eat in the dining facility or, as we used to call it, the "mess hall". Typically, the cooks are up all night preparing a tremendous home cooked meal for soldiers while unit spouses are going the extra mile to decorate the dining area. Unit leaders dress up in their formal uniform and arrive early to thank every cook for their service not only on Thanksgiving but throughout the year and to greet and serve the meal to their soldiers and their families. It is a very special time for soldiers of all ranks to relax and reminisce about home with one another and to celebrate the ending of a special year of soldiering together. As a commanding general of some very large units, Thanksgiving was a wonderful opportunity for me and my strong right arm—my Command Sergeant Major—to travel to every dining facility to visit with our soldiers in a relaxed environment. It was a time to give thanks for our Nation and to personally thank our soldiers for their tireless, dedicated service throughout the year. Thanksgiving was a day to truly connect with leaders, soldiers and their families.

On this Thanksgiving 2016, I hope that you pause to truly connect with your loved ones and to express your thanks to those who work so hard throughout the year to accomplish the most challenging tasks required of them for your outfit to achieve success.

True Growth Reflection: How are you going to bring to life the "thanks" in Thanksgiving this year? Is there anyone from your life story with whom you need to reconnect and thank for all they are doing or have done for you in the past to help you live a life of significance?

For Your Consideration: One way to keep thanks and gratitude at the forefront of your life is to start a daily gratitude Journal. Each morning after you wake or before you end your day list three things or people for which you are grateful.

Recommended Reading: *Living Life as a Thank You: The Transformative Power of Daily Gratitude* by Nina Lesowitz and Mary Beth Sammons
Whatever is given—even a difficult and challenging moment—is a gift. Living as if each day is a thank-you can help transform fear into courage, anger into forgiveness, isolation into belonging, and another's pain into healing.

CHAPTER SEVEN

Matthew's Journey: Embracing Reality, Reinforcing Faith & Family Core Values

SHANE DEVERILL • *June 2015*

LIBBY AND I ARE the proud parents of Matthew. He is our 28 year old nonverbal autistic son who lives with us. He is the older of our two sons. He has challenged us to be a better family and to rise above the daily struggles of parenting a "normal" child, and to accept that our lifelong reality with Matthew would demand a family transformation. Our journey with Matthew transformed our family from a dysfunctional family (trying to survive the moment) into the dysfunctional-functional family (making the best of our new normal and never limiting what might be). Along the way, we endured many trials that deepened our faith, as sometimes that was all we had to survive the moment. These trials (crucibles) expended our physical and emotional energy tanks which caused us to focus inwardly to strengthen our family in order to better help Matthew. Our experience has humbled us, deepened our faith, strengthened our love for one another, and greatly increased our empathy for those with special needs. Here is our story:

We wonder what life for Matthew would have been like had we not traveled around in the military but stayed in one place. At the same time, we think that the upheaval in Matthew's life was good for him as it forced him to be more adaptable to change. We are also grateful for all the different family members, friends, teachers, therapists, and doctors along the way and the various therapies/treatments we discovered that we might have missed had we not traveled.

Matthew was a full-term baby born on October 25, 1986 with no complications during pregnancy or birth. Matthew developed typically as far as we knew until 18-24 months when his language and social skills that should have been developing were nonexistent. He did have chronic ear and respiratory infections beginning at the age of 8 weeks and was on antibiotics constantly. He had four sets of ear tubes beginning at 14 months and ending at age 3 when he had his tonsils and adenoids removed.

Before we had Matthew evaluated, we thought he was just a very independent toddler who loved playing by himself (for hours it seemed). He could organize his blocks by color and stack them over his head-incredible fine motor skills! He also loved lining up his many toy cars and checking out license plates on cars. He was more interested in objects than people, as objects were static and predictable and people were not. When he looked at us, he unemotionally looked through us. As first-time parents, it shook us to our core.

At the age of two we had Matthew evaluated by the Autism Resource Center in Winchester, Virginia mainly for delayed speech. The speech therapist who evaluated him actually came to our quarters at Quantico, Virginia. The therapist believed that Matthew was speech delayed due to his chronic ear problems and not being able to hear well probably most of his life. However, she also detected some auditory processing problems that were not normal for a child that age; Matthew could not follow a simple one-step direction. At this time, we had our second son, Hayden, just before leaving Quantico, and he developed typically with no problems.

We then moved to Ft. Rucker, Alabama when Matthew was 2 ½ years old. There Matthew went through a series of tests including an EEG and CT head scan to rule out any organic causes of his developmental delays. All the tests were normal. Matthew attended a private Christian preschool with typical kids and did fairly well despite biting the other kids when he became frustrated. Matthew began talking at age 3 and said several words . . . mostly functional items like food items, toys, body parts, clothing items, numbers, and letters, etc. He did say, "Daddy" and even a few short sentences like, "Go daddy!" One could not carry on a conversation with Matthew but the words did come out when Matthew wanted to say them. Fortunately, we had close Army friends and family members who insisted on watching Matthew & Hayden so we could get away and recharge-vitally important to maintaining balance with our new normal. These respites allowed us to rest, reconnect, and discuss how to better support one another and Matthew once we returned.

Between Matthew's 3rd and 4th year we explored two different therapies to try and help him. We went to the Option Institute in Sheffield, Massachusetts to learn about the "Son

Rise" program which had supposedly cured Ron Kauffman of his autism. We spent a week learning how to work one-on-one with Matthew to hopefully entice him out of his own world and create situations that would force him to communicate with us (i.e., putting his food up high so he had to "ask" for it.) The program was quite intense and involved recruiting volunteers (friends, neighbors, and several Boy & Girl Scouts) to help so that Matthew could be worked with as many hours as possible per day in his room. The idea was to be so exciting to Matthew that he would want to interact with the volunteers. We were able to continue this program for about a year and a half . . . not quite as intensely as the guidelines called for . . . but at least 4 or 5 hours per day. Matthew did progress during this time and most importantly developed a bond of trust with people that I believe helped him as we explored other therapies later on. He also had daily sensory integration therapy which really seemed to calm him and allow him to focus. We continued to provide the sensory stimulation of deep pressure, swinging, bouncing, spinning, etc. Matthew seemed to need less and less of this stimulation as he aged.

Our next duty station brought us to Ft. Leavenworth, Kansas where we stayed for a year. We continued doing the "Son Rise" program with Matthew 4 or 5 hours a day and he continued in speech therapy. He had a comprehensive evaluation at The University of Kansas Medical Center by a team including a social worker, speech pathologist, psychologist, developmental pediatrician, special education teacher, audiologist, and occupational therapist. After five days of testing, the final diagnosis was moderate to severe autism with possible mental retardation. The diagnosis was emotionally devastating, but through our resilience we decided not to succumb to the expert's assessment but to use the diagnosis to get Matthew enhanced services and to focus on his improvements. During this year, Matthew learned to swim. After several months, he developed an odd stroke that resembled a butterfly less the full forward extension of his arms. Even today he swims the same stroke. Swimming is a great release for him and a shared enjoyment for us as he will look intently into our eyes with complete contentment.

Soon after Matthew's diagnosis of autism, we moved to El Paso, Texas (Libby's hometown) while I did an unaccompanied tour to Korea. We moved there in June 1992 a month after Matthew had his Measles, Mumps & Rubella (MMR) booster shot. During those first few months in El Paso, Matthew's language ceased. To this day we do not know if all the changes in his life caused the regression or if it may have been the MMR booster shot that put his immune system over the edge. The fact is he stopped talking, other than a couple words ("no", "all through") and still does not have speech today. This setback was especially difficult as I was in Korea and unable to comfort and help Libby. Out of desperation, I sought the counsel of our squadron chaplain and a Christian Army buddy-a rarity for me as I did not want to burden others with my problems. They grounded me in enlightening scripture. I began attending church services regularly and started my mornings with the Daily Bread-a great comfort and perspective for me. I returned from Korea to Joint Task Force-Six at Ft. Bliss in El Paso. To my discouragement, I discovered that our younger son Hayden had grown to be both fearful & resentful of Matthew. It was then that I began camping with Hayden. We camped with an Army friend and his son (the same age as Hayden). Our camping trips were a perfect venue to teach Hayden new skills, have fun, and explain Matthew's circumstance. Years later, Hayden apologized for being selfish. I assured him it was all a part of growing up and gaining perspective. Today, Hayden is proud of Matthew. In fact, they both enjoy one another's company and Matthew was Hayden's best man for his wedding.

Matthew was not quite 10 years old when we endured the toughest time ever with him. We survived our typical challenges with him throughout his first 10 years of life: biting, aggression towards his younger brother, smearing his feces all over his room, wandering out of the house naked, hyperactivity, shredding paper and books, and largely ignoring our commands, but when the "rage attacks" as we called them started, we had to do something. It came to a head when we were moving to Ft Drum, New York and Matthew rode with me. He was out of his seatbelt just about the whole time, biting and hitting me from the back seat. When we were not driving he would randomly lash out in a restaurant or our hotel room- not a good situation. This time in Matthew's life was probably the closest we have come to thinking about a residential option for him. He was destroying our family with his behavior, and we were not sure that we could survive the trip let alone having him live at home any longer. It was the lowest point in our family history. It was so bad that I told Libby I didn't know if I could take battalion command as

I could not even drive across country with my family!

Matthew did settle down once we got to New York. He was able to get back into a routine but his aggression and biting did continue. The school district called in a psychologist to evaluate Matthew and to make suggestions for improving his behavior-the answer was communication. We were using the picture communication symbols at the time which seemed to help somewhat. We had tried all forms of communication with Matthew including sign language but he never seemed to take off with any one form.

It was during our first year in New York that we began a true gluten and casein free diet for Matthew. Libby also eliminated soy, corn, and began mega doses of B-6 vitamins. We really did not see remarkable changes in Matthew at home but his teacher did say he seemed much calmer and focused at school. When Matthew turned 12 and was full speed into puberty, he began a new type of "happy aggression" in which he would become aggressive just to say hello to people. His pediatrician recommended we try Risperdal to help even out his raging emotions and hopefully tone down the aggression. We saw an immediate improvement for the first time ever with a drug

In 1999, we spent Matthew's 13th year in Carlisle, Pennsylvania. He attended a regular high school but was in a self-contained class. He was the only student in this class with a teacher and an aide. The teacher had various kids, both special needs and typical, come into the classroom to provide some classmates for him.

The next year (2000), God had bigger plans for us. We moved to Peachtree City, Georgia and I still thank Him for sending us there and connecting us with Matthew's teacher (Paul Batchelor)

for that year. It was probably the best year of Matthew's life. Paul has a gift for teaching special needs kids and he believes in them and expects the world from them. He accepts no bad behaviors, sets limits, and has consequences for misbehaviors and rewards for good behavior. Paul began exploring with Matthew to see what level he might be at academically. Paul discovered that Matthew could read, write, and do simple math problems.

We believe some of these skills were self-taught . . . especially the spelling and math. Matthew continued to amaze us as he quickly learned to tie his shoes, button, snap, and wear a belt . . . all tasks that had never been taught to Matthew as occupational therapists had told us through the years "to keep it simple" and just put Matthew in pull up elastic waist pants and Velcro shoes. We realized the incredible capabilities Matthew had and his teacher was amazed at how quickly Matthew learned the new tasks. The aggressive behaviors diminished greatly and by mid-year, Matthew was attending a regular education science class which he did quite well in: he was able to absorb the information and answer questions over the material accurately. We left Peachtree City after a year and headed back to Ft. Drum, New York with new dreams for Matthew-no limits.

We were happy to be headed back to New York—familiar ground as far as services and schooling for Matthew. We then went to Canada and had a baseline mapping done of Matthew's brain which measured oxygen and blood flow to the various parts of the brain. The scan revealed abnormalities— especially in the temporal lobe responsible for his executive functions (decision making).

We returned to Peachtree City in August 2003 and were thrilled to be reunited with Paul Batchelor. Shortly thereafter, I deployed to Iraq and Matthew became very angry. Despite Matthew's anger, the next few months proved to bring about miracles in Matthew's communication that we had prayed for for years. Matthew began writing (something Paul Batchelor had worked on diligently our first time in Georgia and it had all but disappeared in New York) with facilitation (touch to his hand) to communicate his needs. As time has gone on, he has progressed from writing very basic needs like eat and drink to expressing his feelings and even to being able to express the reason for his feelings. He now wrote in full sentences. He even started to use the words like "please" and "sorry" which was miraculous to us. I am still amazed at the correct spelling and the vocabulary he uses . . . words that his teacher had not introduced! We later learned during his Confirmation class in 2005 that he has a photographic memory. He wrote that it took him 5 seconds to read a page of text. For years he routinely leafed through our magazines, little did we know that he was absorbing information. This communication has opened a whole new world for us and Matthew, as he now has more choices in his life that are not limited to picture communication symbols.

In 2009, Matthew graduated from high school and transitioned to a state sponsored day program called Hands-for-Hire. The program is designed to place special needs individuals in jobs in the local community. Matthew assembles meals for Meals-on-Wheels and does janitorial jobs. He has an IPAD that he uses to communicate. Matthew also sees a neurological chiropractor who has helped him immensely with his concentration, better decision making by discriminating between what he sees and what he hears, proprioceptive processing-in other words co-ordinating input from his senses to deliver effective cognitive information to make better decisions and to better cope in the world. Matthew has developed into an incredibly patient and loving young man who enjoys being with people. In addition to swimming, he now likes biking, running, shooting baskets, kayaking, playing pool, throwing darts, and when Libby's not watching, having an occasional beer with dad! Our next challenge is to plan a transition for Matthew into a group home because someday Libby & I will be unable to care for him. Our fear is an unforeseen event might force a crisis transition.

In conclusion, our journey with Matthew has been one of many peaks and valleys as usually is the case with autism. By embracing our reality and placing our trust in God and not limiting Matthew, we endured many setbacks and are extremely grateful for his progress. Thanks to family, friends, and professionals, we have been able recharge our emotional and physical energy tanks along this lifelong journey. I do believe each therapy and treatment we tried has been worthwhile and many have helped him in one way or another. We now no longer get depressed as each birthday passes for Matthew, as we believe he will continue to surprise us in ways we never imagined. Although we pray for Matthew to speak on his own, I do believe there will be a technological breakthrough to enable his speech in the near future. So, our journey continues . . .

True Growth Takeaway: Never give up hope and never limit outcomes. Embrace your reality and work with family, friends and professionals to make the best for your family. How many opportunities to improve your situation have you avoided because you were too exhausted?

True Growth Reflection: What challenges are you experiencing that demand a reassessment of your core values and a change in your behavior to improve your circumstance?

Recommended Reading: *The Autistic Brain* by Temple Grandin
     "[Grandin's] most insightful work to date . . . The Autistic Brain is something anyone could benefit from reading, and I recommend it to anyone with a personal or professional connection to autism or neurological difference."—John Elder Robison, author of *Look Me in the Eye*

CHAPTER EIGHT

The Last Lap

BYRD BAGGETT • *July 2015*

"One day your life will flash before your eyes. Make sure it's worth watching."—*Gerard Way*

My philosophy in life is to live every minute as if it might be my last and learn like I may live forever. This philosophy was put to the test in June when my wife was diagnosed with stage two breast cancer. Even though the prognosis is positive and Jeanne has an 85% chance of living a healthy and normal life, I realized that I was only living 50% of my philosophy—learning like I may live forever. I'm always reading books on the topics of life and leadership, but I realized last week that I wasn't being true to the most important part of my philosophy—living every minute as if it might be my last.

My nature is that I worry too much about the future—will we have enough money to retire? Will my health hold out? Will my children be ok? Will our business continue to grow? Will Jeanne make a full recovery? And the list goes on and on . . .

Jeanne's diagnosis put things into perspective for me and I am committed to truly living every minute as if it might be my last. Here are a few actions that I'm going to take to live up to the commitment:

- Every morning, list three things or people for which I am grateful.
- Write three handwritten notes every week to people who have positively impacted my life and/or to those who need a dose of hope.
- Don't judge anyone.
- Bring Jeanne flowers every week.
- Cherish the little things that are beautiful about my wife. Tell her and don't take for granted that she knows.
- Meditate every morning for 15 minutes.
- Experience the beauty of Mother Nature by taking a monthly trip to one of Tennessee's beautiful state parks.
- Smile more.
- Pray more.

In closing, I hope this message will inspire you to live your life fully and don't take the next breath or the next minute for granted. As many of you know, I ran track for the University of Texas and believe that a relay race is a great metaphor for life. As you're aware, there are four laps in each relay. Given the assumption that I will live 80 years, each lap represents 20 years of living. Using this metaphor, I'm on my last lap! In the sport of track, the last leg is referred to as the anchor leg, the most important part of the relay, the leg that determines if the team wins a medal. But instead of running faster, I'm going to slow down and enjoy my last lap; I'm truly going to live every minute as if it might be my last! The following poem speaks as to why I'm going to run the last lap with the right pace and grace . . .

Life is a Journey, Not a Destination

Tucked away in our subconscious is an idyllic vision. We see ourselves on a long trip that spans the continent. We are traveling by train. Out the windows we drink in the passing scene of cars on nearby highways, of children waving at a crossing, of cattle grazing on a distant hillside, of smoke pouring from a power plant, or row upon row of corn and wheat, of flatlands and valleys, of mountains and rolling hillsides, of city skylines and village halls.

But uppermost in our minds is the final destination. On a certain day of a certain hour we will pull into the station. Bands will be playing and flags waving. Once we get there, so many wonderful dreams will come true and the pieces of our lives will fit together like a completed jigsaw puzzle. How restlessly we pace the aisles, damning the minutes for loitering—waiting, waiting for the station.

"When we reach the station, that will be it," We cry. "When I'm 16." "When I buy a new 450 Mercedes Benz."

"When I put the last kid through college." "When I have paid off the mortgage." "When I get a promotion." "When I reach the age of retirement, I shall live happily ever after."

Sooner or later we must realize there is no station, no place to arrive at once and for all. The true joy of life is the trip. The station is only a dream. It constantly outdistances us.

It isn't the burdens of today that drive men mad. It is the regrets over yesterday and the fear of tomorrow. Regrets and fear are the twin thieves who rob us of today.

So, stop pacing aisles and counting miles. Instead, climb more mountains, eat more ice cream, go barefoot more often, swim more rivers, smell more roses, watch more sunsets, smile more, hug more, love more, laugh more—cry less. Life must be lived as we go along. The station will come soon enough.

—*Anonymous*

Run the race, your race, the only race you can run, the race you were born to run.

True Growth Takeaway: Live your life to its fullest.

True Growth Reflection: What three actions are you going to take to live a deeper and more meaningful life?

Recommended Reading: *Running to the Mountain* by Jon Katz
   I read this book many years ago and it still remains one of my favorites. Running to the Mountain chronicles Katz's hunger for change

and his search for renewed purpose and meaning. Armed with the writings of Thomas Merton and his two faithful Labradors, he escapes to the mountains of upstate New York where he confronts his life-long questions about spirituality, mortality, and his own self-worth. He ultimately rediscovers a profound appreciation for his work, his family, and the beauty of everyday life—and provides a glorious lesson for us all.

CHAPTER NINE

"Kids Say The Darndest Things" or How I Learned To Listen

Bob Dare • *July 2017*

Take a trip with me to Wiesbaden Germany. The year is 1990; my Son, Matt, is a senior at HH Arnold High School. Matt has done well in school and has proved himself to be academically gifted. He is in receipt of a number of acceptance letters with scholarship offers. He is experiencing the angst associated with college, exacerbated by the fact that he will leave his "home", return to the USA and be separated from his family by an ocean.

I came home from work one evening and as soon as I entered our quarters Matt approached me and indicated that he wanted to talk. I allowed him to complete a couple of sentences before I did a quick mental analysis and determined his "problem", interrupted and began to provide him with "the" solution. I no sooner completed half of a sentence when Matt, in his big person voice commanded, "Shut Up Dad!"

Shocked and caught off guard I began to consider my courses of action. Clearly this was a clean-cut case of insubordination and disrespect. Any good parent would not allow this behavior from a 17-year-old. Do I discipline . . . or do I obey?

As if anticipating my dilemma, in a calmer tone Matt spoke. "Dad, I don't need you to solve anything for me. I will make my own decision. I just want you to listen for once and be a Dad instead of the Sergeant Major."

I sat, looked Matt in the eyes and said, "Sorry Son, go ahead." For the next 15 minutes or so I listened to what my Son had on his mind. When he had finished he came to me, gave me a hug and said, "Thanks for listening Dad, I love you", and then went to his room.

I turned to my wife: "Karen, am I that bad?" She replied without hesitation, "I have tried to tell you for some time that you don't listen. You are too quick to want to solve a problem, and many times people just want an ear. Not everyone is asking for your solution, especially when they haven't even had the opportunity to say what they are trying to say."

Guilty as charged I concluded. And, this was not the first time I had been told that I was too quick to speak. Change was needed and I committed myself to doing so. I stumbled many times and had to begin anew, and even to this day I still have to stop myself from wanting to offer my position or solution before the other person has completed their thought, but I am much improved thanks to a 17-year-old kid who had the courage to speak the truth.

I would imagine that many of you reading this story find it resonating. I do not think that it is always a case of maliciousness when we fail to listen. I think our intent is to help but we fail to take into account the need of the speaker to articulate his/

her thoughts, and we fail to appreciate that sometimes others just want an ear. Listening is an art that is in search of artists. How often do disagreements occur, feelings get hurt or conflicts arise because of poor listening? The True Growth team strongly believes that it is never too late to change. If you are like me and want to improve your listening skills it is not too late to start. It requires discipline, empathy and thoughtfulness. Listening requires one to subordinate oneself to the other person and to refrain from formulating thoughts and responses until you have fully heard and understood the message.

The Fourteenth Dalai Lama said, "When you talk you are only repeating what you already know. If you listen, you may learn something new." And, there is a great Native American proverb that says, "Listen or thy tongue may keep thee deaf."

True Growth Takeaway: Discipline yourself to truly listen when others are talking.

True Growth Reflection: Do I listen with the interest to "hear"? If not, what one behavior do you need to change to do so?

Recommending Reading: *The Lost Art of Listening* by Michael P. Nichols, PHD

Experienced therapist Mike Nichols provides vivid examples, easy-to-learn techniques, and practical exercises for becoming a better listener—and making yourself heard and understood, even in difficult situations.

TRUE GROWTH REFLECTION: TRANSPARENT

Reflect on the following behaviors that are essential to being a Transparent leader:

- The leader's words and actions are consistently aligned.
- The leader openly discusses his/her personal values and the organization's values with others.
- The leader ensures people are informed about the reasons for his/her decisions/actions.

If you need to work on being a more Transparent leader, select the one behavior that needs the most attention and develop three actions that you will work on within the next 30-90 days to shore up this competency:

1. _____

_____

_____

2. _____

_____

_____

3. _____

_____

_____

SECTION THREE

TRUSTWORTHY

CHAPTER TEN

A Value Lost

Bob Hall • *March 2015*

"If put to the pinch, an ounce of loyalty is worth a pound of cleverness."—*Elbert Hubbard*

AFTER RETIRING FROM THE ARMY, I did what I thought was best for me and my family and spent some time chasing dollars before quickly realizing this wasn't what I wanted to do or what I wanted to be. First of all, it took me away from the greatest Americans God put on this earth . . . our Soldiers. I also found that others would willingly ask me to do something that, in my mind, put my integrity in question. Something I always refused to do which caused not a small measure of annoyance to those wanting something I wanted no part of.

Luckily, as I decided on another "life" or career change, I was asked to represent a Fortune 200 company. One that was sincere in their desire to take care of those who served our country in uniform as well as those who had served and their families. I was, once again, around those I loved and respected and was never asked to do anything that put my integrity in question. I felt I was still serving . . . just in a different uniform. But all things change, and ten years later I found that I wanted to be a better husband, father, and grandfather. I wanted to slow down and spend more time with my family, so I decided to retire the second time. And did. Then one day, shopping at Home Depot, the phone rang and I had the opportunity to join a group that allowed me the opportunity to continue to serve. I have now been associated with the True Growth Team for a year and over the Christmas holidays I found myself in a position we would all understand as being on profile.

This gave me time to think and reflect on life and purpose and the Army and personal values. No one has to explain to me, or those of you who have served in the military, the meaning of Loyalty, Duty, Respect, Selfless Service, Honor, Integrity and Personal Courage. Those values are part of our basic character.

While those values are certainly aligned with my personal values, they didn't exactly encompass them perfectly. I, as have you, did the session to identify my personal values and after going through the slide deck . . . I came up with Humility, Moral Courage, Family, Integrity, and Focus on Others.

While at home resting after minor surgery, I thought through those values to decide if they still describe Bob Hall. They do, but maybe they don't do so exactly and that doesn't surprise me. I said during my retirement speech that "I have truly enjoyed my time in the Army and I have no regrets. Certainly there are things I would do differently if I had a chance. And, there are things that I would like to change if I could. But at the end of the day, I can look back at my life and honestly say that I am proud to serve our country as a Soldier." I still feel that way.

Then I think back to my life story, the crucibles that caused me to reflect and eventually to arrive at my purpose statement. During this time of reflection, I heard Chris Carter, NFL Hall of Fame wide receiver, say, "we live in a world of our own experiences."

Certainly that's true, so maybe if I could, I would add the one additional value of "Loyalty" because I lived the loss of that at one point in my life and career.

When I moved into the position as Sergeant Major of the Army, I had a small staff to support me and had decided that I wouldn't change any of the Soldiers now working for me. Each of these Soldiers was experienced, knowledgeable and professional. But, as you can imagine, the key ones received pretty decent job offers because of the access and proximity they enjoyed. When one of my key Non Commissioned Officers told me of a job offer and that while it was attractive, he wanted to stay with me. We talked and he convinced me that was truly his desire. A week later after a trip, I was in the office on a weekend and before I left to head home, I just happened to check to see what had come in on the fax machine.

I read the response to a letter the aforementioned senior Non Commissioned Officer had received for a job offer in which he said that he accepted and could be retired and ready to start two weeks or earlier if they needed him.

I waited and we talked on Tuesday and he tried to explain to me the job wasn't what he had hoped for and the money was for less than he had expected and that he wanted to stay. I explained that wasn't an option. That he could retire and take the offer he initially accepted or he could call Personnel Command (now Human Resources Command), and ask for reassignment. It was emotional for both of us, but I knew I could never rely on his loyalty after this transpired. He retired, took the job, regretted it, and doesn't talk to me to this day.

I guess that's OK with me. I felt (and feel) this was of his own doing and he made the decision, not me. He violated the value of Loyalty by any definition you choose to use and certainly the definition of Loyalty as defined in Army values and in Webster's dictionary.

Did I regret losing him? Of course. Maybe. I don't know. He knew the Pentagon, the people and the systems. But that's okay. I did what I thought then and know now I had to do. Loyalty was too important to me and even now, putting pen to paper here at the kitchen table in the only home Carole and I have ever owned after 19 sets of government quarters, that decision causes me to reflect back on a 4 x 6 card I have kept on my desk ever since my first one in the platoon room in Schwabach, Germany. It states:

"If I were to try to read, much less answer all the attacks made on me, this shop might as well be closed for any other business. I do the very best I know how . . . the very best I can; and I mean to keep doing so to the end. If the end brings me out all right, what's said against me won't amount to anything. If the end brings me out wrong, ten angels swearing I was right would make no difference." That quote is one by Abraham Lincoln. If it's good enough for him, it's certainly good enough for me.

True Growth Takeaway: Never be afraid to re-look where you are and how and what you are doing. Sometimes we have to be willing to face our decisions.

True Growth Reflection: Is there a decision you made because of a conflict of values? What did you do and would you do the same thing if you had a chance to do it again?

Recommended Reading: *Why Should Anyone Be Led by You?* by Rob Goffee and Gareth Jones

In this lively and practical book, Goffee and Jones draw from extensive research to reveal how to hone and deploy your unique leadership assets while managing the inherent tensions at the heart of successful leadership: when to show emotion and when to withhold it, how to get close to followers while maintaining an appropriate role distance, and maintaining your individuality while "conforming enough" to gain traction and lead change. Underscoring the inherently social nature of leadership, the book also explores how leaders can stay attuned to the needs and expectations of followers.

CHAPTER ELEVEN

What Would Coach Think?

Byrd Baggett • *February 2017*

"Self-justification is the beginning of self-destruction."

I **WAS FORTUNATE** to earn a full scholarship to participate in track and field at the University of Texas in Austin. During my career, I was a four-year letterman, was on two Southwest Conference Championship teams, was elected captain my junior and senior years, and was an All American. Even though I am proud of these accomplishments, what I am most grateful for is the leadership lesson that I learned from my head coach, Jack Patterson.

Coach Patterson recruited me and was the head coach during my freshman year at UT. Even though it was many years ago—1968 to be exact—I can distinctly remember the day Coach Pat visited my home in Pasadena, Texas to offer me a scholarship. My parents were not home at the time but my grandmother, who was living with us, was present during Coach's visit. After he left, my grandmother, a tough and wise lady from East Texas, turned to me and stated, "Bubba, that's a good man and you better sign that scholarship offer!"

If you talk to any athlete who was fortunate to have been on one of his teams at Merkel High School, San Angelo High School, the University of Houston, Baylor, and Texas, I'm confident that the majority, if not all, would say that he was a man of integrity who never compromised his core principles. He was a true man of God and, without proselytizing, lived his life accordingly. When Coach was recruiting athletes, integrity of character always came before talent.

After my freshman year, Coach Patterson went back to Baylor where he served as the Director of Athletics from 1971 until his retirement in 1980. In his first year, he hired Grant Teaff, another man of impeccable integrity, as head football coach and, three years later, Baylor won its first SWC football title in 50 years. For his many accomplishments as a coach and administrator, Coach Pat was elected to the Texas Sports Hall of Fame, the Drake Relays Hall of Fame, as well as the Baylor University and Rice University Athletics Halls of Fame. In my opinion, his greatest accomplishment was that he never placed winning above integrity and would be so saddened at what a wholesale lack of integrity has done to the reputation of his beloved Baylor University.

I'm confident that none of this would have happened if Coach Pat was at the helm, as he would NEVER allow his staff, coaches and athletes to place winning above integrity—his conscience would not have allowed such. The following words, from one the world's most admired leaders, speak to Jack Patterson's legacy:

"When you lose your wealth, you lose nothing. When you lose your health, you lose something. When you lose your character, you lose everything."—*Billy Graham*

True Growth Takeaway: Integrity is a choice. It is consistently choosing the purity of truth over popularity.

True Growth Reflection: Is there any part of your life where you are compromising your integrity? If so, what do you need to do to fix this part of your character?

Recommending Reading: *Lead with Humility: 12 Leadership Lessons from Pope Francis* by Jeffrey A. Krames

When Fortune announced its list of the World's Greatest Leaders in 2014, the top spot was awarded— not to a captain of industry—but to the new pontiff.

Since his election, Pope Francis has earned that accolade . . . and more. He has achieved the remarkable: breathed life into an aging institution, reinvigorated a global base, and created real hope for the future. How did a man who spent his life laboring in slums far from the Vatican manage to do this and so quickly? The answer lies in his humility—and the simple principles that spring from it. Lead with Humility explores 12 of these principles and shows how leaders and managers can adapt them for the workplace with equally impressive results.

CHAPTER TWELVE

Trust: The First Phase of Combating Divisiveness

BYRON BAGBY • *December 2016*

> "Trust is the highest form of human motivation. It brings out the very best in people."—*Stephen R. Covey*

"**T**RUST" IS MORE THAN the root word for trusting and trustworthiness. Trust is the foundation of any meaningful relationship between and amongst family members, co-workers, friends and organizations.

When I think of the word trust, one person that immediately comes to mind is Mr. Overton T. Harris. Mr. Harris was born, raised, educated and employed in Fulton, Missouri. His family has been in the banking industry since the 1850's. Over a period of more than 60 years, he performed many roles at The Callaway Bank from teller to President/Chief Executive Officer and Chairman of the Board.

Mr. Harris' life and mine have a lot of similarities with both of us being: natives of Fulton, Missouri; graduates of Fulton High School and Westminster College; and members of the

Westminster Board of Trustees. Yet, we have some dissimilarities which one could see as a barrier to building trust. One difference is both of my parents were relegated to domestic work and unskilled labor because they were barred from attending Fulton High School due to racial discrimination. Whereas Mr. Harris' family enjoyed open-ended opportunities.

When I was a junior at Westminster College, Mr. Harris was Senior Vice President of The Callaway Bank and lectured at one of my upper level economics classes called "Money and Banking." At the end of his lecture, he gave each student a business card and said to call or stop by the bank to see him if he could ever do anything for us.

A year later, toward the end of my senior year, I wanted to buy a car. At that time, I did not have a regular job, and had no savings nor credit history. Neither of my parents were in a position to co-sign for a loan. I remembered the offer Mr. Harris made to my classmates and me a year earlier, and made an appointment to see him. I went to his office at The Callaway Bank and explained what I wanted. Without hesitation, he told me to find the car I wanted, write a check for the purchase price, and bring the bill of sale to him the next business day and we'd complete the necessary paperwork for the loan. I found a late model used car, wrote a check for the purchase as Mr. Harris directed and took the paperwork to him the next day. We worked out the loan details that were to my satisfaction. It became apparent to me that Mr. Harris recognized my trustworthiness.

We've all heard the phrase "trust, but verify." I'm wise enough to know that before Mr. Harris gave me his trust, he verified my graduation status and that I was going into the active Army a few months later. Earlier, he had tracked my progression as a young African American man who had taken advantage of available opportunities to improve my life. As a bank officer for one of the largest banks in Central Missouri to grant a car loan to a young man with no credit history, no job, no savings and no one to co- sign for the loan was one of the greatest examples of trust that I've seen in my life. Mr. Harris looked beyond the color of my skin and disadvantaged upbringing to allow me to earn his trust. I'm not saying that life's playing field is completely level. Because most likely subconsciously or unintentionally, I am pre-judged, stereotyped and profiled more often than you realize. But, if more people would follow the example set by Mr. Harris to be more trusting and recognize the trustworthiness of others, our world would be less divisive.

Mr. Harris moved into an assisted living facility in early 2015. The last time I visited with him was in April to have a cup of coffee. He passed away two months ago at the age of 88.

True Growth Takeaway: In a trusting relationship, the trustor is responsible for taking risks, and the trustee is equally responsible for being trustworthy. When both parties fulfill their respective roles, a state of trust exists. This is true for relationships between and amongst individuals and organizations, in all sectors of our society.

True Growth Reflection: Do I place trust in others as a prerequisite to earning theirs? How do the best leaders build trust? How can I be more trustworthy?

Recommended Reading: *The Speed of Trust*—Stephen M.R. Covey
From Stephen R. Covey's eldest son comes a revolutionary new path towards productivity and satisfaction. For business leaders and public figures in any arena, *The Speed of Trust* offers an unprecedented and eminently practical look at exactly how trust functions in our every transaction and relationship

CHAPTER THIRTEEN

The Consequence of Lost Trust

BYRD BAGGETT • *June 2017*

SEVERAL YEARS AGO, I was having a discussion with one of my clients, interviewing him concerning the topics he wanted me to cover in an upcoming talk I was going to give to his sales team. He singled out integrity as one of the areas he wanted me to emphasize in my presentation.

This client then went on to tell me about one of his peers, an executive in charge of another manufacturing division. This senior manager and two sales representatives were making a sales call on a long-term client. It was a relationship that had accounted for most of the division's sales volume. After that meeting was over, the executive noticed that one of their competitor's new product samples had been left behind for the client to evaluate. Thinking they were alone in the room, the executive placed the sample in his briefcase, closed it, and took the sample home to evaluate.

It turns out, however, that the executive and his two sales reps had not been alone in the room. One of the client's representatives had walked back into the room unnoticed and seen the executive swipe the sample. As a consequence of this lack of integrity, both sales representatives were fired and the executive was barred for life from calling on this customer. Millions of dollars in business and a long- term relationship were lost because of one bad error in judgment! This sad but true story is the basis for another of my favorite quotes: "Trust, once lost, is almost impossible to regain."

As this story illustrates, integrity is the foundation for true success in both our personal and professional lives. A life fulfilled is wisdom lived, not knowledge learned. Your journey will not be easy, and your choices may not be popular, but your steadfast commitment to the purity of truth will separate you from the mass of mediocrity. Always search for the truth and never compromise, and the richest blessings of life will be yours.

True Growth Takeaway: Trust takes months to earn but minutes to lose.

True Growth Reflection: Are you consistently trustworthy? If not, what behavior do you need to change to be so?

Recommending Reading: *Crucial Accountability: Tools for Resolving Violated Expectations, Broken Commitments, and Bad Behavior*— Patterson, Grenny, McMillan, Switzler, Maxfield.

This is an excellent resource for improving relationships in the workplace and in life.

CHAPTER FOURTEEN

A Matter of Trust

Bob Dare • *November 2015*

TRUST IS THE FOUNDATION for any positive relationship, whether it is an organization, a military unit and even a family. Trust is a choice one makes. When we board a commercial airliner, we trust that the crew is dedicated, professional and competent. When we visit our doctor, we trust that he/she is able to accurately diagnose our malady. When we hire a technician to service our heating or air conditioning we trust that the report he renders, and the bill he provides, reflects the truth associated with his services. There are a number of other examples I could cite but I think the point is clear, trust is a necessity.

I am a very trusting person, and to a fault my wife reminds me. I rarely count the change I receive. I take people at their word. I believe that the vast majority of people are honest, want to do a good job and prefer the Golden Rule over dishonesty and distrust. It is a choice I have made for some time and it is what makes me rise each day and greet life with a smile and optimism.

Some years ago, I was privileged to serve in the US Army's

ceremonial unit, The Old Guard, (TOG). The Soldiers of TOG are charged with performing a myriad of highly visible ceremonies from posting our Nation's Colors to providing the final salute and honors to those deceased Soldiers and their family members. The caring, attention to detail, commitment and professionalism that must be displayed daily by those honored to serve in TOG cannot be understated.

I stood near my new company commander one morning as we dispatched squads and platoons in numerous directions to perform those ceremonies I mentioned above. I knew these Soldiers. They were trained and dedicated. I trusted them.

"First Sergeant", said the young Captain, "Who is checking on these squad leaders and team leaders? How do we know they will not screw up their mission?"

"Captain", I replied, "Every day we take off our rank and hand it to these Soldiers. We send them out all around Washington DC. There are a thousand things that can go wrong, all of which will cause the two of us great discomfort and unwanted attention. I have been here for 30 months and the one thing I can tell you is that each day when the vans and buses return our troops, they return with our rank intact, safe and sound. You have to trust them Sir."

Those Soldiers never fractured the trust I had for them. Their behavior reinforced in me that when you trust others, they will deliver. A trusting environment engenders positive performance. This does not mean mistakes will not be made. Mistakes occur, but I have found that when you trust first, the mistakes are minimal and honest, and the manner in which you mitigate those mistakes is instructive and constructive rather than demeaning and retaliatory.

Trust is not without risk. Trust is like a fine piece of crystal, when it is cracked it is gone, and it is expensive to replace. I have had only a few people who have fooled me and have lost my trust. It is disappointing when this happens, but it has not changed my conviction and my choice to first trust. I look for the good in everyone and every experience. When disappointment hits, trust gives me the strength to accept it, learn from it and to positively move on.

True Growth Takeaway: When you trust more, you get more.

True Growth Reflection: Who do you distrust? Why?

Recommended Reading: *The Speed of Trust* by Stephen M.R. Covey
Written by the eldest son of Stephen R. Covey, The Speed of Trust offers an unprecedented and eminently practical look at exactly how trust functions in our every transaction and relationship-from the most personal to the broadest, most indirect interaction-and how to establish trust immediately so that you and your organization can forego the time-killing, bureaucratic check-and-balance processes so often deployed in lieu of actual trust. Read this book if you're interested in taking your personal and professional relationships to a new level.

TRUE GROWTH REFLECTION: TRUSTWORTHY

Reflect on the following behaviors that are essential to being a Trustworthy leader:

- The leader acts with integrity, i.e., does what is right, regardless of his/her personal feelings.
- The leader makes every effort to deliver on promises and commitments.
- The leader willingly admits his/her mistakes and accepts complete responsibility for his/her actions.

If you need to work on being a more Trustworthy leader, select the one behavior that needs the most attention and develop three actions that you will work on within the next 30-90 days to shore up this competency:

1. _____

_____

_____

2. _____

_____

_____

3. _____

_____

_____

SECTION FOUR

APPROACHABLE

CHAPTER FIFTEEN

The Moral Courage to Challenge Others

Lawson Magruder • *September 2015*

OVER THE LAST FEW YEARS we have been reading about one scandal after another where senior leaders in both the civilian and military ranks have demonstrated poor judgment through inappropriate conduct. Each time I read about one of these scandals, I wonder how long this went on and who knew about it and failed to confront the senior leader or report the behavior to higher authority. Each scandal has resulted in a stain on the senior leader's institution, public embarrassment, some form of punishment, and career derailment. In each instance, sadly I suspect, there were superiors, subordinates and peers along the way who turned a blind eye to what was going on and did not have the moral courage to challenge their business associate or friend to stop the inappropriate behavior.

I suspect we each have known someone who has suffered a derailment that could have been stopped if we or someone else had stepped in to challenge the leader. The saddest case I witnessed was a senior military leader- a peer general officer- whose career was terminated due to alcoholism and then he sadly died within months of his retirement. Through the years since his passing, I have heard many state that they knew he was a heavy drinker even at an early age but "he always got the job done to a very high standard". I have always wondered how many should have intervened along the way? A superior? A peer? A CSM? A subordinate? Perhaps it would have fractured their relationship but have inspired him to change his destructive behavior.

The courage to challenge others is a behavior that we ask to be assessed on our Authentic Leader 360 Assessment. Typically, respondents focus on the leader's ability to challenge subordinates or direct reports, not their courage to challenge a superior or supervisor. Usually the excuse given for not challenging senior leaders is fear of retribution, a severe reaction, denial or rejection. How many of us failed to challenge a superior in the past and then later found out that the leader ended up heading down the path of self-destruction, career derailment, a divorce, serious health issue, and an extremely adverse impact on junior leaders' careers, the team's morale, and mission accomplishment? How many of us look in our rear-view mirror with regret that we did not have the courage, the guts to give timely advice to a friend, a business associate or a senior leader when we observed self-destructive behavior? To a friend who was living beyond their means? To a friend who was abusing alcohol or drugs? To a peer who was pressing the envelope with verbal or physical abuse of others? To a superior who was having an inappropriate relationship with the spouse of a subordinate or peer? Perhaps because we didn't intervene in a timely matter, the leader got on the slippery slope of self-destruction and to the point of no return. Regrets, we have all had a few.

The questions that we should all be pondering are:

How can we prevent ourselves from the path of self-destruction and how can we approach someone we know is heading in the wrong direction?

Here are a few tips:

Self-Protection:

- Place your True Growth model in a prominent place in your office to periodically grade yourself on how you're living your own personal values which are the nucleus of your character.

- Have a confidant/ombudsman/"watchdog" in your life who can come into your space at any time and provide feedback and advice to you. You must be open to feedback.

- Frequently look yourself in the mirror and ask the question: "Am I bringing honor to myself, my family and/or my organization with my actions?" If the answer is "no", then you need to change your behavior immediately. Perhaps you will need the help of a professional to address an issue like an addiction.

- Periodically ask for feedback from your direct reports on your behavior. Challenge them to challenge you when your behavior is inappropriate and not in alignment with your organizational and personal values. Ask for anonymous feedback on specific behaviors. Perhaps a good place to start is with the questions on our 360 Assessment. Ask for a "+"/Delta on your behaviors.

Helping Others:

- Before you approach the leader, ensure you have specifics to share with them. If you have personally observed the inappropriate behavior, you need to provide the time, place and specifics.

- If you have been provided information from another about a friend or leader in your chain of command, you need to corroborate the information before you confront the leader.

- If you need assistance in delivering the message to a superior, perhaps a peer of his or her may be of assistance in carrying the message. A tough call to take it outside your chain of command but it may work better.

- Your feedback needs to be timely and provided in private.

- If you feel like the behavior is putting the unit's mission and it's personnel at risk, you are obligated to pass the observation on to the next leader in your chain for his/her action.

- You must realize that the initial reaction of the leader may be anger, emotion or rejection but oftentimes you will have planted the seed for immediate change of their behavior. Hopefully they will thank you someday for "saving them from themselves"!

True Growth Takeaway: You need to have the moral courage to challenge a friend or business associate who is heading for derailment because of inappropriate behavior.

True Growth Reflection: Is there a friend or business associate in your life right now that needs to be challenged to change their inappropriate behavior before it results in personal embarrassment or negatively impacting the unit's mission or possible derailment of their career? If so, what steps do you need to take to help your friend?

Recommended Reading: *The Road to Character* by David Brooks

Blending psychology, politics, spirituality, and confessional, *The Road to Character* provides an opportunity for us to rethink our priorities, and strive to build rich inner lives marked by humility and moral depth.

CHAPTER SIXTEEN

Toothpaste & Toilet Paper

Bob Dare • *February 2014*

In 1990 my family and I were stationed in Germany. We resided in a stairwell apartment best described as cozy. There may have been a total of 850 square feet including three bedrooms and one bath. My son had begun his senior year of high school, my daughter, her sophomore year. There were a number of rules that had been established and compliance was expected by all. Two of those rules had been decreed by me and were non-negotiable; never squeeze the toothpaste from the center of the tube, and never leave the toilet paper holder empty.

There came a time when the frequency of violation of these "important" rules surpassed my level of tolerance. When noticed, I lost all sense of reasonable self-control, raising my voice to a level of a scream and leveling threats that went beyond the death penalty. It seemed that time after time I would enter the bathroom and there in plain view was the toothpaste tube clearly squeezed from the center portion. As if that were not enough to ruin my day, the only visible evidence of toilet paper on the holder was the cardboard spool! The audacity of my family! Why were these two simple rules consistently violated? Was this is a test of my role as head of the household? The obvious disrespect could not be tolerated, so the very next time that I entered the scene of the recurring crime I really exploded. My voice seemed to shake the walls of the apartment, my body convulsing in anger. I ranted for about 10 minutes. I could not get anyone to respond. My daughter calmly shut her bedroom door, my wife continued to be busy in the kitchen acting as if I were nothing more than a character on the TV.

The door to my son's room opened and Matt approached me cautiously but deliberately. "Dad, can I talk to you?" I immediately began to think, what can a 17 year old high school senior possibly say that could reduce my angst and turmoil? I acquiesced.

"Dad, we are not your soldiers and this is silly, so silly that I have been purposely denting the toothpaste tube and removing the toilet paper and putting the empty roll on just to see your reaction. I am speaking for everyone when I say neither of these things is that important for you to blow up like you do. If you were to die in combat, I would be sad but I could explain it, but if you have a heart attack over toothpaste or toilet paper what could I say to people?" (Is feedback a gift or what?)

Oh the honesty and candidness of youth! I had been taken to school by my son. Similar to the Grinch, who experienced heart growth when he learned the true spirit of Christmas, I underwent a comfort zone growth beyond description as reality smacked me in the face. It was not so much that my rules were incorrect, but my reactions were flawed. As I thought about the wisdom in my son's message I wondered how many other things and times did I react with rage and loss of emotion? The change in me was immediate and everlasting. I began to step back from moments of heightened emotions and considered the importance and the impact of my reaction. I worked hard to keep things in perspective. I was sensitive to the fact that my reactions had impact on others and not always the impact that I wanted. I reevaluated "important" and violations of toothpaste and toilet paper rules no longer rated a priority in my life.

True Growth Takeaway: It's important that we not let negative emotions control our actions. There is wisdom in thinking about the consequences of our words before we speak.

True Growth Reflection: Do you sometimes let negative emotions rule you? If so, what one behavior can you improve to keep them under control?

Recommended Reading: *The Only Way to Win* by Jim Loehr

If you only read one book this year on personal and professional development, we highly recommend "*The Only Way to Win*" by Jim Loehr, a world-renowned performance psychologist. It is full of practical and applicable insights that will help you on your journey to significance. For those of you who have read Jim's best-seller, "The Power of Full Engagement", you will find this book as impactful.

CHAPTER SEVENTEEN

Taming Technology

DAN ELDER • *August 2015*

IN THIS CONNECTED WORLD today's military leaders may often find themselves distracted in a sea of technology. One moment we are turning on our first computer with excitement and the next we are juggling multiple unit-issued phones, tablets and personal devices, computer email on multiple secure open and private networks, and social media requirements that can all lead to "digital distraction." We all know the importance of face-to-face communication. Soldiers and leaders of our organizations expect our presence at key and important activities, so how can we "Tame the Technology Demon" and complete our required digital tasks while still leaving time to direct and lead our units?

The "killer app" and one of the biggest time sucks we are often faced with is electronic mail and text messages, with instant messaging not far behind. The allure of electronic mail is a double- edged sword because as effective and efficient that it can be to transmit and respond to information, it also can end up taking up a lot of your time both in and out of the office.

We as leaders take pride in our abilities to understand, visualize, describe, and assess our operational environments, but it is often the day-to-day routine things that we do without a lot of thought that eat up our valuable time and energy. Maybe your digital activities are in need of an energy audit to see if you are expending the right amount? I don't know about you, but I never really had much in the way of a formal class on electronic mail in any of my military and civilian education programs. I just did it and it wasn't very complicated.

If after your own assessment you feel you could use a few tips to better discipline yourself, then here are a few from author Dr. Geraldine Markel that she shares in her book, *Actions Against Distractions: Managing Your Scattered, Disorganized, and Forgetful Mind.* I concur with her theory that we find ourselves getting consumed by what she calls the "technology demon." She seems to recognize that we do not have to be draconian in our approach, but to create some rules and parameters around technology to help us try to gain back some of our time. A few recommendations that may prove useful to busy leaders are:

- Be ruthless. Immediately delete and unsubscribe from any unwanted newsletter or announcement feeds.

- Establish a decision-making system by deciding what actions are warranted for each message: e.g., delete, archive, and file by category for response at a later date, schedule as a work task, read and respond to immediately.

- Organize. Create a filing system and use color-coded tags

to store or archive categories of e-mail (e.g., travel, legal, committees, or organizations).

- Be timely. Schedule fifteen- to thirty-minute periods to prioritize and schedule tasks first thing in the morning or the night before.

- Postpone. Put low priority materials, such as newsletters, reports, or training, in a folder and schedule a limited weekly time to review them.

- Use the subject line to summarize your message to make it easier for others to process your mail. Ask them to do the same when they send you e-mails.

- Avoid using your e-mail inbox as a to-do list. Instead, as soon as you see a task that needs doing schedule time on your calendar to work on it.

- Use social support. Discuss the problem with peers and family; with their help, identity ways to deal with time-wasting e-mails.

In the end, emails and text messages are not likely to stop, and the devices like cell phones, tablets and computers are too important to how we live. But instead of just showing up at a place, we each should create our own individual plan by taking some time to develop our own personal approach to taming the demon.

True Growth Takeaway: "Technology is nothing. What's important is that you have a faith in people, that they're basically good and smart, and if you give them tools, they'll do wonderful things with them." —*Steve Jobs*

True Growth Reflection: What is the right amount of time you believe you should dedicate per day on email, and must you change any behaviors to achieve that goal?

Recommended Reading: *Actions Against Distractions: Managing Your Scattered, Disorganized, and Forgetful Mind* by Dr. Geraldine Markel
Drawing on the author's years as a trainer and coach, Markel's book provides a step-by-step guide to banning common distractions from work/life. It provides a 5-step plan of attack and 7 strategies to implement an action plan against common distractions such as technology, interruptions, an unruly mind, stress and fatigue.

CHAPTER EIGHTEEN

What If We Really Cared?

Bob Dare • *March 2017*

> Humankind has not woven the web of life. We are but one
> thread within it. Whatever we do to the web, we do to our-
> selves. All things are bound together. All things connect.
> —*Chief Seattle*

I have the quote above in a small picture frame positioned on my
desk where I cannot avoid reading it each day. Chief Seattle of
the Suquamish Tribe spoke those words over 150 years ago. His
words addressed the rapidity in which the Nation was expand-
ing without regard to the impact the expansion was having on
peoples and the environment. I do not think that his concerns,
expressed so profoundly above, have lost relevancy.

The negative effects of not realizing that we are all part of
"the web" often results in actions predicated on "what's best for
me". How will this affect me? What does this do for me? Will this
work to my benefit? We don't always take the time to consider
that our behaviors are not always restricted in scope and impact. We want that tree limb resting on our lawn to be gone so

we relocate it to the neighbor's property. We are unhappy with the latest policy that management has issued so we engage in water cooler gossip in an attempt to build dissent, rather than approaching the source and addressing our dissatisfaction professionally. We hear a tasteless joke and think it is funny so we tweet it out to a larger audience without regard to the potential hurt it may cause. We walk or drive by someone in need because we are in a hurry to take care of our own business, and besides, "someone else will help."

There are countless examples I could provide but the point is clear, "All things connect". What we do or not do does impact others. Without thinking critically, responsibly and with empathy before we act, we can very well create an unintended consequence that causes hurt or suffering. When we allow our emotions to be unchecked we can often do or say something that, although regrettable, it nevertheless is done, and the damage cannot be repaired. Too often we use freedom and privacy as "licensing" to serve a selfish cause.

Perhaps it is time for a little comity to enter our lives. Comity can be found in the Golden Rule, or in Rousseau's "social contract", or, as the ancient Romans called it, *civitatis filia*, civic friendship. How much improved might the challenges of today be if we were to truly consider the total reach and effect of our behavior? What if we agreed with Chief Seattle, "whatever we do the web, we do to ourselves", and realized that each one of us, in our actions and words, directly or indirectly, impacts this planet and those around us? What if we really cared?

We cannot deny the fact that humans are social animals

and are not supposed to be alone. We need one and another. We are all connected. What we do to "the web" we do to each other. If each of us were to genuinely care, practice empathy when making decisions, if we remain cognizant that we are "but one thread" within the "web of life", then it seems to me that we would enjoy a robust and meaningful life. We will never eliminate all evil and disappointment, but, we can make our space in this world a better place.

True Growth Takeaway: We need each other.

True Growth Reflection: What small act of kindness can I share today?

Recommended Reading: *Learned Optimism: How to Change Your Mind and Your Life* by Martin Seligman.

Without knowing it, most of us impose limits on our achievement and our happiness by approaching life's problems and challenges with unnecessary pessimism. Dr. Seligman, the father of positive psychology and a pioneer in cognitive psychology and motivational research, tells you how to identify your own self-defeating thought patterns —and how to harness the powers of your conscious mind to break those patterns.

TRUE GROWTH REFLECTION: APPROACHABLE

Reflect on the following behaviors that are essential to being an Approachable leader:

- The leader acts in a self-assured way and is comfortable engaging in conversation.
- The leader encourages others to provide feedback to improve his/her performance and the organization's performance. Is receptive to negative information, i.e., does not "shoot messengers".
- The leader demonstrates the courage to challenge others.
- The leader is frequently visible throughout the workplace.

If you need to work on being a more Approachable leader, select the one behavior that needs the most attention and develop three actions that you will work on within the next 30-90 days to shore up this competency:

1. _____

_____

_____

2. _____

_____

_____

3. _____

_____

_____

SECTION FIVE

PURPOSEFUL

CHAPTER NINETEEN

Lost, In A Lost World©

BOB DARE • *September 2016*

THE SONG TITLE ABOVE was made popular in the late 1960s by the Moody Blues. The lyrics tell of troubled times, of the violence and unrest that the World was experiencing and of the trepidation associated with being lost, in a lost world.

The thought occurred to me that many of us may feel today that we are lost, in a lost world. Do you? It is so easy today to become Chicken Little and declare that the sky is falling. But is it? Are the significant events of today any more traumatic to us now, than the significant events were to those in times past?

No doubt that each of us can evaluate the current events against our personal values and conclude that there is "trouble in River City", but that is old and continuing news that will survive each of us. Life is one doggone crucible after another, some personal, some societal, some global. I read a lot of history and am always amazed that the World has survived the past events that it has. I am sure that often, those who lived through those many troubled times felt lost, in a lost world.

Of course, there are differences between the past and present, one in particular, technology. Technology has shrunk our World in both time and space. We now see in real time, critical and sometimes horrific events that in the past took hours or even days to be reported. And we see it "on location", and we see it over, and over, and over again; and, depending on our points of view, we are able to select how those events are reported to us, inclusive of slanted and biased opinions and sound bites that in many ways distract us from the "news", and create a demand for instantaneous answers to questions requiring facts; facts that require time before any accurate answer can be rendered. Many of us who served in the military understand that, "the first report is always incomplete and inaccurate." The late William Manchester, one of our great historians, said that history written prior to 25 years following any event is normally premature and usually contains errors and inaccuracies created by the injection of emotion and a lack of research and knowledge of facts.

In many ways, we have allowed ourselves to become impatient and demanding for immediate resolution and accounting. We have access to data that are miles wide but only an inch deep. Many of us fall prey to the idea that for everything there is a rational and known cause, therefore there is an immediate and everlasting solution. And so, we become lost, in a lost world.

Would you like out? I don't have a patent on a map but there are three ideas I will share with you that guide me daily. Maybe these three ideas will help provide you with a "GPS" that you can use to journey out of your lost world.

First: Change the way you think! We choose to adopt our thoughts but, we are different from all other living beings in that we have choice. Quit thinking the worse. Spend just a little time in a history book and I am sure that you will learn that every era that mankind has survived was replete with crucibles and challenges and some were pretty gloomy and ugly. Give thought to the good that exists, there is plenty of it! If you choose to change the way you think, you will change the way that you are! Buck O'Neil, one of the greatest baseball figures who played the game, played his entire career in the Negro Leagues. He was being interviewed late in his life by a young reporter. The two were attending a professional game so that the reporter could get Buck's perspective on the modern game. A foul ball was descending into a young fan's hands when an older fan jumped between the young person and the ball, caught it and went back to his seat. "Buck, did you see that?" asked the reporter, "That guy took that ball away from that little guy! That's horrible!" Buck replied, "Oh, maybe he has a little boy who will really appreciate the ball." The reporter thought for a moment then asked, "Well, if he has a little boy why isn't he here at the game?" Without hesitation Buck responded, "Maybe he is home sick and the ball will help him feel better." Try as people might, no one could get Buck O'Neil to think ill of others, particularly when he did not know the facts. We could all learn from that story.

Second: If you are going to use your energy, why not use it on something that you can control, something for which you are informed and knowledgeable, something for which you can make a difference. It makes more sense to me to concentrate my efforts within my circle of influence, and although I allocate time in my circle of interest, I refuse to dwell there, because being informed, and being involved are two completely different things, but both require energy. I know very few people who have much influence within their circle of interest but spend an awful lot of their time focused there, while things within their circle of influence go neglected. I make it a point to listen to the news once during the day. I do so in the morning and then I am done for the day, the exception being if a major event occurs. I am very confident that should it come to pass that "the sky is falling" someone will let me know and even then, there will not be much I can do so I am certainly not going to burn precious energy thinking or worrying about it.

Third: Grab hold of some spirituality and don't let go! There is enormous research that concludes that even the biggest skeptics cannot rid themselves of the inner thought that there is something bigger than themselves and reaches beyond the here and now. It is inherent in us to question, to wonder and to contemplate. I think the first step in gaining spirituality is accepting that in of ourselves we are nothing. We need something much more than "me". Our journey through life is so miniscule but requires direction and meaning that alone, we cannot provide. Many people rely on their religion for their spirituality; for others, it is found during personal mediation or deep thinking; for some it is one's "lighthouse of the soul" always searching, always there to guide and protect. Spirituality, a lot like faith, is the answer to "why" when there seems to be no other answer; it allows one to weather the storms of life and grow from each experience; it provides that inner peace that we all desire. Spirituality allows us to survive our crucibles and be better rather than bitter.

Being lost, in a lost world is a choice. You do not have to wander without hope or optimism. Begin today to find a route to a better, happier you. Life is too short to not enjoy its blessings and bounties. Make a decision to change today, and if you are one of many people who are not lost, help someone that is.

True Growth Takeaway: Spend your energy in your circle of influence; don't get distracted by things for which you have no control.

True Growth Reflection: Am I lost, in a lost world? Why?

Recommended Reading: *The Power of Positive Thinking* by Norman Vincent Peale

An international bestseller with over five million copies in print, *The Power of Positive Thinking* has helped men and women around the world achieve fulfillment in their lives through Dr. Peale's powerful message of faith and inspiration. With the practical techniques outlined in this book, you can energize your life-and give yourself the initiative needed to carry out your ambitions and hopes.

CHAPTER TWENTY

Kenny's Story

BYRD BAGGETT • *September 2014*

"Nothing in the world can take the place of persistence. Talent will not; nothing is more common than unsuccessful men with talent. Genius will not; unrewarded genius is almost a proverb. Education will not; the world is full of educated derelicts. Persistence and determination alone are omnipotent. The slogan "Press On!" has solved and always will solve the problems of the human race."—*Calvin Coolidge*

A FRIEND OF MINE, Kenneth Tedford, tells a childhood story. Kenny was declared "mentally retarded" in his earlier years. His mother, an alcoholic, died when Kenny was 8 years old. His adoptive mother loved him, but his adoptive father was embarrassed to have him around. One day, during a class in elementary school, the teacher asked the children to draw a stick picture depicting what they wanted to be when they grew up.

Pictures of doctors, nurses, policemen and firemen were posted all around the room. Kenny's picture was one with the "stick" person standing next to a podium with an American

Flag in the background. When Kenny explained that he wanted to be a motivational speaker and make people feel good, the teacher responded, "But Kenny you know you can't do that, you're retarded!"

Kenny's response was, "Well, you're a teacher and you're not real smart!" The teacher immediately sent Kenny to the principal's office for punishment. The teacher explained the situation and left Kenny alone with the principal. The principal got down on one knee and, looking directly into Kenny's eyes, stated, "Kenny, that teacher is a very cruel person, and I know that you can be whatever you dream to be."

Later, during a series of tests, Kenny was found to be legally deaf, not retarded. Kenny is now a successful motivational speaker, stand-up comedian and has authored several children's books!

True Growth Takeaway: Don't quit before the blessing!

True Growth Reflection: In what area of your life do you need to be more resilient? If Kenny could, you can!

Recommended Reading: *The Obstacle is The Way* by Ryan Holiday
The tag line—"The Timeless Art of Turning Trials into Triumph" speaks to why you should give this book consideration.

CHAPTER TWENTY-ONE

Running for The Kids

GREG BATTON & BYRD BAGGETT • *June 2014*

"A hero is someone who has given his or her life to something bigger than oneself."—*Joseph Campbell*

I WANT TO SHARE the following story written by Greg Batton about my friend, Gary Welch . . .

A human tendency is to believe that we will always go from point A to point B in a straight, logical line. But there are no straight lines in nature. Why then do we think our lives will be the exception? Look around you right now. Where are you in life? How did you get there? If you are anything like me, you marvel at the crazy journey that has deposited you here. Here's another quick nature lesson. You can tell the age of a creek by the number of bends and twists. Younger creeks are straighter than older ones.

Through the years the water erodes the sides and creates a wonderfully interesting work of nature. I think people are like that too. The older we get, the more turns we can look back on. At least that's true of the more interesting folks among us.

The reason I am so obsessed with lines and turns and jour-
neys has to do with a mission that started twenty-five years ago:
the Memphis to Peoria Run for St. Jude. For 25 years individuals
have given of their time and energy to run the 465 miles in order
to raise money for kids with cancer. While the line on the map
between Memphis and Peoria remains the same year after year,
no one can ever anticipate what the run will do to their lives.
Talk about changing your plan—that run will do it.

One such changed runner is Gary Welch. Gary turned to
running only to help Dick Versace, former Bradley basketball
coach, get ready for a charity run. He liked the way running made
him feel, and it became part of his life. In 1990, some friends
suggested that Gary take part in the St. Jude run. Thinking it
would be a great ego booster to be able to tell his friends and
colleagues that he ran from Memphis to Peoria, he agreed. In his
mind, the journey was mapped out. Make the run, raise some
money for sick kids, get the congrats and pats on the back, and
move on. What Welch didn't count on was meeting the kids
in Memphis prior to starting the run. "I didn't know that we
would be visiting the kids at St. Jude's in Memphis before we
got started,"he says. "It changed everything. No longer was this
about running. It was about helping."

Welch had encountered his first bend in the road. And the
bends kept coming. Year after year, Welch and countless others
like him would dedicate a little more time to raising funds for
the St. Jude run as day after day the images of sick children stuck
in their minds. It wasn't until 1995 that the big, loop-de- loop,

cloverleaf bend occurred in Welch's life. Gary was attending a personal development conference on the East Coast. He was telling the Memphis to Peoria Run for St. Jude story to Dr. George Sheehan, author of Personal Best. Dr. Sheehan tossed Gary another curve in the form of a challenge. "Why not run for those kids every day?" asked Sheehan. Stunned by the challenge, Welch returned home in the fall of 1995 and could think of nothing else. Could he do it? Should he do it? Yes. Was it crazy? Probably.

On January 1, 1996, Gary Welch announced to his friends and family that he would run one hour every day for the kids at St. Jude. He hasn't missed a day since. Not one. As of this writing, he has run 3,244 days in a row. To add to the remarkable nature of this accomplishment, Welch has never been injured. And I should mention that he's 61 years old.

I asked Welch to explain why he thought he was able to run injury free and he couldn't really answer. My explanation is that when you are engaging your mind in something that you truly, deep down in your soul believe in, your body will protect itself. It's a team effort: body, mind, and spirit. The commitment that Welch and so many others in this community have made to the kids of St. Jude is also a team effort; runners, contributors, and organizers. The success of the St. Jude run, like Welch's experiences, could never have been predicted. The bends and turns in this creek are many. And as those who have participated over the past 25 years can attest, it has been a wonderful journey. Lives have been changed.

There is a very poignant sign hanging over Gary Welch's

office door. As you exit the room, you can't help but read it. "Either you ran today or you didn't." He knows that that sign is not just about running. It's about commitment. And it applies to all of us.

I challenge you to get passionately engaged in something greater than self. That one commitment will keep hope alive for others and will allow you to live a life of significance.

True Growth Takeaway: Get passionately engaged in something greater than self and the true riches of life will follow.

True Growth Reflection: What one commitment can you make to improve the lives of others?

Recommended Reading: *The 12th Angel* by Og Mandino
This story about a Little League baseball player will touch your heart and challenge you to "pay it forward". This story so touched me that I purchased 50 copies one Christmas for friends and family members.

CHAPTER TWENTY-TWO

"Why Are You Here?"

LAWSON W. MAGRUDER III • *April 2014*

BATTALION COMMAND is the pinnacle for many military officers in their careers and I relished every day I spent leading America's finest young men and women.

In January 1985, I had been in battalion command for 19 months and knew that the completion of my two years in command was rapidly approaching. The culminating event was a major winter training exercise focused on the defense of Alaska. My light infantry/airborne outfit had been given the primary missions focused on defense of the critical nodes on the Alaska pipeline. We had trained quite hard for this mission for several months and I was very confident that we would succeed.

On the second day of this three-week exercise, I received an emergency phone call from my sister Anne in Austin, Texas. She told me over the phone that our Mom had gone into ICU with respiratory issues and I needed to come home. I explained to her that I was on a training exercise but she insisted that I needed to come home. After I hung up the phone, I told my wife Gloria about the phone call and she immediately said you need to go tell your brigade commander (my immediate supervisor) and your Commanding General that you need to catch a plane immediately and head home. I told Gloria I had a difficult time believing the severity of Mom's illness and that I could go see her when the exercise was over. Gloria insisted that I needed to go home. But after hearing this sage advice from my precious wife, I still thought I was too valuable to my unit to be gone during this exercise. So, I went to see my brigade commander and told him about the phone call and he said "you do what you need to do Lawson and I will support you." I then went up to see our Commanding General, Brigadier General Jerry Bethke. Jerry knew me well as I had worked for him in a Ranger battalion many years prior. I figured he would agree with the brigade commander and leave it up to me.

I confidently walked into Jerry Bethke's office and told him about the phone call from my sister and fully expected him to endorse any decision I made. To my surprise, he looked me in the eyes and said "Lawson, why are you here? Why would you question your sister and Gloria's judgment? You get on a plane immediately and go home to your Mom. She needs you at her side right now. That's your primary mission in life right now, not this training exercise. We're going to truly find out how good your battalion is while you're gone. You have trained them well and I predict they will excel in your absence. Move out and catch a plane immediately."

The next day I obeyed my General's "order" and I flew home to Austin. The next five days were a very special time for our family as we sat in the hospital room supporting Dad and reminiscing and expressing our love to Mom. On the fourth day, Mom seemed to be out of the woods and doing much better. She told each of us to head back to our families and me to my training exercise. I said a tearful farewell and returned to Alaska. Within a couple of hours of my return, Anne called me again and said that Mom had passed away.

I've often wondered, what if I had not returned to Austin to be with Mom. What guilt and regret I would've carried with me to this day if a compassionate, understanding Jerry Bethke had not asked me: "Why are you here?"

PS—In my absence, my beloved Warrior Battalion under the command of my executive officer excelled on the exercise.

True Growth Takeaway: Success at the expense of family relationships is really failure.

True Growth Reflection: How can you ensure in the future that your self-interests and ego don't get in the way of the much higher priority of focusing on the needs of others? Particularly those you love.

Recommended Reading: *How Will You Measure Your Life?* By Clayton Christensen

What a challenging question, "How will you measure your life?" As the back cover states, "This book doesn't offer easy answers. Instead, it will prompt you to consider the most important questions you'll ever face. It won't tell you what to think. Instead, it aims to teach you how to think-about your life and your purpose-by sharing powerful research and theories about success and failure that were developed at Harvard Business School and other institutions." This book will help you understand how to make the critical decisions that can bring happiness and success into your life. It's another must read!

CHAPTER TWENTY-THREE

Hope in America

PHIL JOHNDROW • *March 2014*

WHEN I WAS IN BAGHDAD, IRAQ and a Brigade Command Sergeant Major, I met two Iraqi translators, Afrah and Lina AL Asadi. I originally knew their names as WHY and BECAUSE. Whenever I saw these two young women, they were always positive and upbeat and were committed to making a positive difference in their country. As I learned more about them, I was touched by how much they loved their country and the depth of their commitment to make it a safer place to live. I knew some men who would not take the chances they took because of the danger involved. Here you had two women who willingly took on that kind of danger every day.

Because of the danger to themselves and their families, they took different routes to and from our post so they would not be followed and harmed. They told me how they had to tell everyone that they worked for another company and not the U.S. Army.

Several other translators who worked with us were killed; some in attacks on our convoys and others were executed. Each of these workers was critical, as they provided us with the ability to communicate daily with the Iraqi people and dignitaries. They were force multipliers and we could not conduct our mission without them.

When I came back to Baghdad as the Division Command Sergeant Major, I went on a routine combat patrol to their camp and noticed that the girls were not there. My heart dropped when I was informed that they had been attacked for the second time. During the attack, one broke her ankle and the other had some burns on her back, but the good news is that both were going to survive.

At the time, there was a program that allowed us to send selected Iraqis who had served with us, and whose lives were in danger, back to the United States.

These women had completed the paperwork but it was stalled at the Brigade headquarters and needed to get to Division headquarters to be approved by a General Officer. I went to brigade and picked up the paperwork and personally took it to one of our Generals. He asked me if I trusted them. My response, "with my life!" He never asked another question, as he could see in my eyes the determination that I was never going to let anyone hurt these young ladies again. I was so happy that I was able to get them out of Iraq and that they could lead safe and productive lives in the United States. The big surprise was when I was told that I was their sponsor and was personally responsible for their care for the first year in the United States. This included a place to live, food, clothing, etc. I was still in Iraq and communicated to my mother that she was going to have "some guests for dinner" and she took the women in.

Think about the adjustment that these young women had to make—from 120 degrees in Iraq to being relocated to my home state of Montana where it can be as cold as 10 degrees below zero with snow, which they had never seen. They not only accepted, but they thrived amidst the many adjustments they had to make to assimilate into the American lifestyle; such changes were nothing compared to worrying about their lives in Iraq.

During a conversation with a Vietnam veteran who was still deeply troubled for not doing something for the brave Vietnamese who risked their lives for him and his fellow soldiers, he promised that he would help Afrah and Lina get jobs and look after their well-being. And that he did.

The girls have lived in Montana for the past 6 years and have adjusted well to their new home. The best news is they passed the naturalization test and are now proud citizens of the United States of America. I never felt more proud when I joined them in reciting the Pledge of Allegiance as they waved their American Flags during the ceremony. Words cannot express how blessed I felt to be part of such a happy ending.

I will never forget the moment they thanked me for saving their lives and I then thanked them for saving mine.

True Growth Takeaway: People can live 40 days without food, 4 days without water, but only 4 seconds without hope. There's no greater feeling than keeping hope alive in others.

True Growth Reflection: What can you do today to give hope to one who is hurting?

Recommended Reading: *Unbroken: A World War II Story of Survival, Resilience, and Redemption*

In this book, Laura Hillenbrand chronicles the life of Lieutenant Louis Zamperini. It is one of the most emotional and inspiring books of survival that you will ever read. As People magazine stated, "Staggering . . . mesmerizing . . . Hillenbrand's writing is so ferociously cinematic, the events she describes so incredible, you don't dare take your eyes off the page."

CHAPTER TWENTY-FOUR

Mindful Monkey, Happy Panda©

Bob Dare • *February 2015*

KAREN AND **I** SPENT **C**HRISTMAS with my son Matt and his family. Matt has this uncanny ability to read body language and facial features. I have always been challenged with the exercise of patience and it becomes visible when I begin to stress or allow my mind to wander from the task at hand. When "multi- tasking" was introduced into our jargon, I had a perfectly legitimate response when I was accused of not having my head in the game. So, here we were with my Son, his wife Jacci and my granddaughters, Eleanor and Alice, enjoying the holidays. The perfect time for relaxing, unwinding and concentrating on family.

On day three of the visit, during the early afternoon, while engaged in a rousing game of hide-and-seek with Eleanor and Alice, Matt observed me checking my email.

"What are you doing Dad?" asked Matt.

"Multi-tasking Son. Getting a little work done while . . ."

Matt interrupted, "Dad, there are a number of recent studies that I could provide you that opine that multi-tasking is not possible. Your brain allows you to focus on one thing at a time, that is, if the one thing is your task at hand and you intend to do it well. I have noticed that you seem to be unable to just do one thing for very long until you start planning the next thing that you are going to do. I am betting that this is a major contributor to your fatigue and your stress. If you are going to play with the kids, play with them. If you are going to work, tell them that that is more important right now. They will understand."

Busted, right then and there. I had no retort, no good answer. Once again I was forced to realize that my lack of patience and ability to devote myself to slowing down, enjoying the moment, and "being there" was having a negative impact on me and others around me. I put away the phone and disciplined myself to the task at hand; hide-and-seek.

About an hour later Matt delivered to me a children's book, the title? Mindful Monkey, Happy Panda©. Here is the paraphrased abridged version:

The mindful monkey cannot understand why the panda is so happy every time they meet. The monkey engages in many of the same daily tasks as the panda; exercise, reading, playing, etc. At the end of each day the monkey is exhausted and unfulfilled. The panda is all smiles, energetic, upbeat and positive. The monkey finally decides to query the Panda:

"I don't understand, states Monkey, I do everything that you do but never feel rewarded." "What do you think of when you are doing something?" asks Panda.

Monkey replies that he thinks about the next thing or things he is going to do (see where I am going with this?)

Panda cheerfully states, "When I am reading I only think of what I am reading, when I am walking I think only of the benefits of my walk, and when I am . . . "

I think you get the lesson of the story. I have thanked Matt a number of times for providing me a child's book that is so instructive. I now mentally call upon the story to keep me focused on what I am doing at any particular time. It's never too late to learn, is it?

*Mindful Monkey, Happy Panda© Lauren Alderfer & Kerry Lee Maclean

---

True Growth Takeaway: How many things do we miss at the moment because we are not fully engaged in what we are doing? How much energy do we waste by trying to spread our minds over numerous things simultaneously? How many conversations are lost because, instead of listening, we are formulating our words?

True Growth Reflection: How can I get more out of each special moment?

Recommended Reading: *Mindful Monkey, Happy Panda*
This wonderful picture book for children and adults alike introduces the powerful practice of mindfulness in a fun and exciting way.

CHAPTER TWENTY-FIVE

Mother's Day Disaster— Is Finding Balance Possible?

KEN KEEN • *August 2016*

ACHIEVING WORK-LIFE BALANCE is easy for leaders to talk about, but rarely easy to execute. The importance of achieving work-life balance was highlighted in a 2015 report on Millennials from the U.S. Chamber of Commerce; it found that three out of four Millennials reported that work-life balance drives their career choices.

On 12 May 1996, I received a phone call from my Regimental Commander asking "What is today?" I quickly responded, 'Sunday.' He went on, "I know that, but what is today and what are you doing?" I went on to explain to him I was in the field with the Battalion and we were doing a company live-fire exercise. Of course, he knew that, so he reminded me it was also 'Mother's Day' and I was failing miserably to lead by example ... giving me some very candid and honest feedback. Why had I decided to be in the field on Mother's Day? Surely, we could have planned around it. I had failed to find the right balance into one of our core values of "Mission First, People Always".

A few weeks ago, my wife and I saw my former Regimental Commander and his wife, the first thing he asked was whether I had ever made up for the "Mother's Day Disaster". It was a memory I preferred to suppress, but one I had carried with me since then and reminded myself of often over the years.

Admittedly, I was never very good at this, but this moment had often reminded me of "I could and should do better for my family and those I serve."

The former Vice Chairman and COO of Coca-Cola said this about balance, "Imagine life as a game in which you are juggling some five balls in the air. You name them-work, family, health, friends and spirit and you're keeping all of these in the air. You will soon understand that work is a rubber ball. If you drop it, it will bounce back. But the other four balls-family, health, friends, and spirit-are made of glass. If you drop one of these, they will be irrevocably scuffed, marked, nicked, damaged, or even shattered.

They will never be the same. You must understand that and strive for balance in your life."

In looking back on my Army career, I was blessed to only have been scuffed and marked up for my failing to achieve better balance between Soldiering, family, friends, and spirit.

So, what can we do to achieve a better work-life balance and what does it really mean? If it were easy, it would not be one of the major areas most leaders struggle with where many rate themselves in 360 surveys as needing improvement.

It takes constant work, open communication with your leaders, family, friends, and developing a climate where feedback is welcome, and you must lead by example. I still struggle to get this right and seek self- improvement with the help of my family and friends. Here are some ideas that others have offered for consideration:

Manage your time with balance in mind. Look at your calendar over the course of a day, week, and month.

Take your full vacation time and insist that others do the same. Honor weekends, national holidays, AND Mother's Day.

Come to work at a decent hour, and leave at a decent hour. Make sure your team knows you aren't going to reward workaholics.

Respect your leaders and teammates' time. Don't send emails on the weekends. Save the drafts when a great idea strikes you, just wait until the next work day to send them. If you absolutely must talk with of one your leaders or team members during off duty hours, send them a text with the subject and ask them to call you when they're free so they have time to wrap up what they are doing.

Celebrate people, families, birthdays, life achievements. Your team will feel you value them as people.

Finally, with respect to balance between our work and family, it is not about the quantity of time we spend with them, but the quality. A counter argument to the work-life balance is what Matthew Kelly argues in his book "Off Balance". He says work-life balance is a myth, that they cannot be separated, saying it is about effectiveness and having "a satisfying experience of life". It is worth considering as we seek to achieve readiness in our organizations, however we can only define what constitutes a satisfying experience of life for ourselves, not for others.

True Growth Takeaway: Achieving balance in life is difficult; it takes constant work by leaders at every level.

True Growth Reflection: What can you do to achieve better balance or a satisfying life experience?

Recommended Reading: *Off Balance* by Matthew Kelly

Kelly lays out the system he uses with his clients, his team, and himself to find deep, long-term satisfaction both personally and professionally. He introduces us to the three philosophies of our age that are dragging us down. He shows us how to cultivate the energy that will give us enough battery power for everything we need and want to do. And finally, in five clear steps, he shows us how to use his Personal & Professional Satisfaction System to establish and honor our biggest priorities, even if we spend a lot more time on some of the lesser ones.

CHAPTER TWENTY-SIX

Faith, as a Source of Strength

BOB DARE • *April 2016*

IF YOU ARE LIKE ME, you occasionally struggle with living. There are a number of negative distractors to life, but those distractors exist and we cannot pretend that they don't; nor can we eliminate them. Some things, as bad as they are, have always been and always will be. Crime, violence, tragedy, failure, disappointment, and other unwanted events are part of reality. This is not to excuse bad or evil behavior. We must, when we can, properly correct those events wrought by human failure, but to think that we can make them go away is to engage in wishful thinking. I believe the real secret to surviving the rigors of life is reliance on faith.

What is faith? For the purpose of this narrative I cite the following definition: "Belief that does not rest on logical proof or material evidence." For some, faith is synonymous with religion. For others it may be that internal GPS always guiding you. And for others, it is that mystical, spiritual belief that all things cannot be explained or controlled, but, "that's okay".

Regardless of the source, for those who possess faith, I am

sure you would agree that faith allows one to accept that there is not an answer to every question, nor a rational explanation to every event; science, including medical science, cannot eliminate every challenge; mankind cannot and does not control everything.

Faith provides the ability to cope with the pains and frustrations that are inevitable in this world. Faith provides the strength to rise and return to the fight of life after we have been knocked down by a right hook from reality. Faith provides resilience to weather those disasters and sorrows that life's storms leave in its aftermath. And faith provides the moral courage that protects us from group-think, and causes us to choose that harder right over the easier wrong.

My experience tells me that you normally can identify people of faith. They seem happy, smile more often, show genuine concern and care for others, and see the good that is prevalent in our world. They understand that they cannot "fix" everything and they accept that "life is what's happening while we are making other plans."

Faith is not hard to find. It exists in each of us. It is a choice one makes to believe in a higher power rather than engage in self-aggrandizement. Faith can be the foundation upon which one can build a powerful and determined psyche. Faith is not Pollyannaish; it is not denial or ignorance towards life's distractors mentioned above. Faith provides the positive motivation that gets us up and propels us forward when times are tough.

Some time ago I read what became, and remains my daily mantra: "Do the best you can; leave the rest to faith."

True Growth Takeaway: Do the best you can; leave the rest to faith.

True Growth Reflection: What can I do to strengthen my faith?

Recommended Reading: *Care of the Soul* by Thomas Moore

Basing his writing on the ancient model of "care of the soul"-which provided a religious context for viewing the everyday events of life-Moore brings "care of the soul" into the twenty-first century. Promising to deepen and broaden the readers' perspectives on their life experiences, Moore draws on his own life as a therapist practicing "care of the soul," as well as his studies of the world's religions and his work in music and art, to create this inspirational guide that examines the connections between spirituality and the problems of individuals and society.

CHAPTER TWENTY-SEVEN

Rock & Roll Legacy

BILL WEBER • *February 2016*

As WE AGE AND MOVE through the seasons of growth in our lives, the thoughts of how and what we will be remembered for occupies more and more of our time. What do you want your family and others to recall about you years after you pass as they sit around the table thinking and talking about you? And what legacy will you leave?

For example, I spoke with a former senior Army leader shortly after he had retired who was in the process of setting up college investment accounts for each of his 11 grandchildren (at the time) with the intent to fund each of their college educations in the future. I walked away thinking what a noble idea that was, one that would be remembered and have a significant, lasting impact on his family for generations to come.

That discussion led me to start thinking about other examples and how I think of others and myself. How do actions influence perceptions and what will be remembered? What can I do now and in the future to be remembered as someone that made a difference? The following story relates another example, a powerful lesson that people do change and are not always what you think they are.

While assigned to the Army Staff, my spouse, Robin, volunteered to assist the USO escorting celebrities on various visits to Walter Reed and Bethesda. On one occasion, she was escorting a quite famous entertainer who was on her first visit to the hospitals. This was during a period of the Iraq war when casualties were high and we had dozens of severely wounded filling the hospital wards.

Despite the warnings that what she would see would be unsettling and difficult, until she walked into the first room, she could not really conceptualize how bad it would be. Entering the first room, the intense shock of seeing bloodied, damaged, and bandaged Soldiers with tubes, needles, bags we are so familiar with was overwhelming. She connected the best way she could with the injured and their families without breaking down until she moved back into the hallway to cry and then recompose herself before entering the next room.

She continued her visit well past the time allotted and it had such a tremendous personal impact on her that she wrote 10 pages in her daily journal and shared the experience with her mother, who she spoke with every day for 3 hours. The next night she stopped her concert before 25,000 people and described in tears the impact the hospital visits had made on her; transforming her from a carefree, never married, cavalier person with few responsibilities into a mother, aunt, sister, and friend to those who needed her. She truly was transformed and determined to make a difference.

She then began visiting on a frequent basis, passing out MP3s loaded with music and connecting with our wounded and their families in a tremendously noble way, clearly moving into a season of significance. I tell this story when we talk about legacy and a LTC I was coaching told me he knew immediately who I was talking about because he was his unit's LNO (Liason Officer) to Bethesda and saw her late one night running the hallways. Incredulous, he asked the staff about her and they told him that she was essentially a member of the staff and was allowed to come and go when she pleased without escort. She never wanted any notice or attention for her actions; she truly was one of us, serving in her own way.

I still get choked up telling this story, a story that demonstrates that perceptions of people may be inaccurate or ill-informed and that people will surprise you. I'll never forget what Stevie Nicks did (and still does as far as I know)—she certainly earned the highest degree of respect and honor from those she touched and when I think about her legacy and what I would put on her tombstone, it would be: SHE CARED. I only hope others will think the same of me.

True Growth Takeaway: There is nothing more rewarding than being a part of something greater than self.

True Growth Reflection: If you died today, how would your sentence of life end?? With a period (.), question mark (?), or exclamation point (!)???

Recommended Reading: *Leaving a Legacy: An Inspirational Guide to Taking Action and Making a Difference* by Jim Paluch

Something magical happens when 7 characters from every walk of life decide they can make better use of their time as they sit around McDonalds every morning, by sharing the wisdom they've gained through the years rather than their disappointments and complaints with life. As they learn the magic of the Redbud tree and rally to help a little crippled boy, wonderful things begin to happen. Seven great pieces of wisdom are shared with the reader as the characters start a movement of senior citizens across the country that literally changes everyone's perception of aging. In this heart-warming, life changing story, readers young and old will realize it's never too early or late to apply wisdom, take action and make a difference.

CHAPTER TWENTY-EIGHT

Life versus Livelihood

Bob Dare • *May 2017*

HARRY CHAPIN WAS A BALLADEER. He wrote a number of songs that spoke of life, living, people and relationships. One of my favorites is "Mr Tanner". It is a story of a humble man in the Midwest who is a drycleaner. Mr Tanner is happy with his profession but he is also gifted with the talent to sing. The local people persuade him "to pursue music fulltime." He finally capitulates but in the end the attempt fails because of a professional critic who is unkind in his review of Mr Tanner's ability. My favorite line of "Mr Tanner" is, "Music was his life, it was not his livelihood". Mr Tanner returns to his dry-cleaning business and to singing as his passion and, as the lyrics say, " . . . . he sang from his heart, and he sang from his soul.

He did not know how well he sang, it just made him whole."

I was listening to "Mr Tanner" the other day and it occurred to me that probably there are many of us who have a talent, a capability, a "life" that does not connect to what we have chosen for our livelihood, but unlike Mr Tanner who was perfectly content with dry-cleaning and found personal joy in his singing, we allow our livelihood to be our "life". We make plans to enjoy our "life" just as soon as _____. (You can fill in the blank)

The problem is that while we are mired in our livelihood, before we know it we have missed opportunity after opportunity to experience the joy, happiness and rewards that are found in our "life". Unlike Mr Tanner, we can't find the balance needed to enjoy each day as we should. We find temporary outlets that we believe will provide relief from "the grind" but we soon grow tired or lose interest as we "have to" give priority to making a living. Before we know it, days become weeks, weeks become months and months become years and our livelihood has stolen our life.

So, let me ask you, what is your "life"? Is it balanced with your livelihood? Is there a hidden talent or desire inside you that you have been holding back until, "just as soon as _____."? Is there something you can give or do that will bring you real joy, happiness and sense of worth? I believe that each of us has the ability to do something special, to make a meaningful difference. We just have to take a moment, step back from our daily routines and be introspective. Wouldn't it be a shame if after we have departed this world others are heard remarking, "He was always going to do that just as soon as _____."?

Why not take the steps now to ensure that those words are never spoken of you? Don't let your livelihood rule your life. It is never too late to make a positive change that will bring happiness and joy to you and those around you.

True Growth Takeaway: Don't let your livelihood keep you from living your life.

True Growth Reflection: Are you living your life? If not, what changes do you need to make?

Recommended Reading: Read, or reread, *The Purpose Driven Life* by Rick Warren.

This book became and remains the bestselling hardcover non-fiction book in history and has now tallied over 32 million sales. It is the second most translated book after the Bible.

CHAPTER TWENTY-NINE

My New Year's Resolution: Simplicity

Byrd Baggett • *January 2017*

As we all prepare to embrace the opportunities, promises and potential challenges of a new year, I would like to share my goal for the next 12 months: I am committed to spending my time, energy and resources to living a year of simplicity.

This commitment came as the result of several weeks of reflection in December. As I was looking in the rear-view mirror of my life, reflecting on the many joys and challenges of my 67 years on this earth, it occurred to me that true happiness has everything to do with living a life of simplicity. The years when I focused too much on materialism were never fulfilling—just a never-ending pursuit of more.

When I was a young boy, during the Christmas season, it was a tradition that our family would leave our modest home in Pasadena, Texas and drive into the wealthy suburbs of Houston to admire the beautiful lights and decorations. In my adult years, my Dad used to remind me that I would ask him "Daddy, why can't we have the big homes and cars that these people have?" His response was, "Son, if you work hard in class and get a college degree, you can have these nice things." The truth? When I got the things I never had, what I had was never enough. It took me many years to understand that "more" wasn't the answer. If you're not careful, the more things you have, the more things can have you.

In my life, I have discovered that the older I get, the wiser my parents were. One of the greatest gifts that my Dad gave me and my sisters was a journal that he started in 2001 after he had moved into his home on Canyon Lake north of San Antonio, Texas. Daddy didn't have more than $20,000 in savings when he died, but he was the happiest and most authentic person that I have ever known.

I'll let the following words from his journal tell "the rest of the story".

"Hello kiddos. Well, I'm sitting on my back porch overlooking the Suche Valley with the beautiful Texas Hills in the background. When I first moved here Christmas of 2001, I was the 2nd one to move in on the ranch. Thanks to my children, I am able to live out the rest of my life in the beautiful Texas Hill Country. I guess I fell in love with it back when my father took me hunting on the Dittmar Ranch about a hundred miles north of here at Doss, Texas. That was 1936 and I was 12 years old. I climbed up on one of those points overlooking the valley and the hills and I said right then one of these days I hope I can live in these beautiful hills. So, my dream has come true thanks to my children. When I first moved here, all you were able to see was the cedar, live oaks, the valley, hills, a windmill and tank, the ruins of an old rock school where I guess the old settlers' kids, back in the 1800's, went to school and an old German cemetery about 100 yards from the school. Now there are about 25 or 30 houses you can see dotting the hills and the valley. Can't blame the people for wanting to live here though. Well, I'm starting at the end, so now I want to give you a little bit of what I know about the Baggett family . . .

When typing these words from Dad's journal, I could feel his smile and gratitude. He never complained and had few wants—he loved his family and God and that was enough to sustain him through a tough life. He was born in a tent during the Great Depression, lost an infant son, lost his wife at the tender age of 57 and survived a major heart attack. He had many reasons to be bitter but he made a conscious choice to live life through the windshield, not the rear-view mirror. He was a simple man who lived a simple life and made a positive difference in many lives. That's a legacy of significance.

Thanks, Dad for your inspiration and wisdom. I'm a better man, father and husband because of you.

True Growth Takeaway: There is freedom in simplicity.

True Growth Reflection: What do you need to do to live a life of simplicity?

Recommending Reading: *Enough & This Could Help* by Patrick Rhone
I had never heard of this author until I watched the *Minimalism* documentary. As a result, I purchased his book, *Enough* and encourage you to do the same—great resource on how to live a life of simplicity.

TRUE GROWTH REFLECTION: PURPOSEFUL

Reflect on the following behaviors that are essential to being a Purposeful leader:

- The leader demonstrates the importance of an effective work/life balance between career, family, and self.

- The leader openly shares his/her life's calling (purpose).

- The leader encourages his/her people to consider their future and to ensure they are fueling their calling in life.

- The leader seeks to continuously improve his/her performance.

- The leader ensures that everyone understands that competently completing their responsibilities is essential to achieving the team's mission.

- The leader lives the principle that real success is helping others to be successful while the organization accomplishes the mission.

If you need to work on being a more Purposeful leader, select the one behavior that needs the most attention and develop three actions that you will work on within the next 30-90 days to shore up this competency:

1. _____

_____

_____

2. _____

_____

_____

3. _____

_____

_____

SECTION SIX

RESPECTS/VALUES PEOPLE

CHAPTER THIRTY

What Coach Taught Me About Leadership

BYRD BAGGETT • *October 2014*

"If your actions inspire others to dream more, learn more,
do more, and become more, you are a leader."
—*John Quincy Adams*

I HAVE IDENTIFIED four characteristics of the world's most authentic and effective leaders:

Number One: They truly care about their followers.

Number Two: They have an unconditional belief in those they lead.

Number Three: They are fair. They have the same standards for all.

Number Four: They expect excellence—in all thoughts, words, and actions—from each team member.

Great leaders like Tom Landry (Dallas Cowboys), Mary Kay

Ash (Mary Kay Cosmetics), Mother Teresa, Herb Kelleher (Southwest Airlines), and Cleburne Price genuinely care about their followers. With the exception of Cleburne Price, the previously mentioned individuals are universally recognized as great leaders.

Cleburne Price, Jr. was one of the most influential people in my life. His guidance helped me achieve both athletic and academic excellence at the University of Texas. Most importantly, the lessons that he taught me from 1968 through 1972 have helped me become a better man, both personally and professionally. The "how" can best be illustrated by sharing two conversations that I had with Coach, one during my freshman year and the other during my senior year.

The year was 1968. The place was the University of Texas. It was my freshman year at the university that I had always dreamed of attending. I had achieved a goal of a full athletic scholarship at the flagship university in the state of Texas. I was a small-town boy, a celebrated high school student athlete who was totally lost on the huge campus in Austin, Texas. My vision of being a contributor on the Texas Track Team looked bleak, as there were many sprinters and quarter-milers that had run times much faster than my high school bests. I cried myself to sleep the first several months and truly wanted to return to the comforts of home. Here's where the first conversation with Coach Price occurred. He asked to see me, an unproven freshman, in his office one day after practice. I was puzzled, as I was new and didn't know why Coach wanted to meet with me.

Here's the essence of the first conversation—I arrived at Coach's office and he asked me to sit down. I was a little intimidated, being a freshman and worried that something must be wrong for Coach to want to personally visit with me. He said, "Byrd, I am very proud to have you on our team." I'm thinking, "He really cares about me." He went on to say, "Byrd, I have several goals for you. Number one is that you are going to be a four-year letterman." My thoughts, "He really believes in me!" He continued by saying, "We are going to win at least one Southwest Conference Championship and I am counting on you to help make this happen." My thoughts, "How can I let this man down, as he truly cares and believes in me?" Next, he said, "I truly believe that you have the talents to become an All American." My thoughts, "I am an unproven freshman and he believes that I will become one of the best runners in the country." Finally, he concluded our meeting stating, "Byrd, my final expectation is that you will be elected captain by your teammates." I don't think I need to tell you what I was thinking. My thoughts of quitting the team had vanished because of one conversation with this man. I couldn't wait for the next day's practice!

Coach's words proved prophetic, as we more than achieved his predictions. I lettered four years, was on two Southwest Conference Championship teams, was elected captain of the team for two years, and earned All American honors by being a member of the world's fastest sprint medley team in 1971.

Following is the second conversation that was held in Coach Price's office after my senior year of 1972—As with the first conversation, Coach had asked to visit with me in his office. I had graduated and my thoughts were focused on making it in the business world. Like my freshman year, I was a little intimidated and worried about my future. I sat in the same chair and looked across at Coach Price. I will never forget the pride and compassion in his eyes, as he said, "Byrd, we did it." He recounted the two conference championships, my earning four varsity letters, the world-class relay race in which I became an All American, and the distinction of being elected captain during my junior and senior years.

He continued with words that will forever be in my heart. "Byrd, I have never coached an athlete that hated to lose more than you. You worked harder than any athlete that I have had the privilege to coach." He got up and moved around the corner of his desk and asked me to stand up. He hugged me and, with a tear flowing down his cheek, said, "You know how I feel."

I am blessed to have many great leaders who have influenced my life. Thanks to all for caring and believing in me.

How about reaching out to that one person who has made a positive difference in your life? That call might just make their day.

And Coach, "You know how I feel."

True Growth Takeaway: Belief in self is critical for one to achieve their full potential.

True Growth Reflection: What three people have had the most positive influence on your life? Call or visit them and let them know how you feel; don't assume they know. What individual do you know who needs someone to believe in them? What about reaching out and being that person?

Recommended Reading: *Synchronicity: The Inner Path of Leadership* by Joseph Jaworski

This is simply one of the best books that you will ever read on how to become a more authentic leader. Put this at the top of your list!

CHAPTER THIRTY-ONE

The Question I Get Asked the Most

Vinny Boles • *August 2014*

BEING A PROFESSIONAL SPEAKER on the subject of leadership is a great way to make a living and as a side benefit you meet an interesting cast of characters on a regular basis in some great locations.

The question I hear most often in the Question and Answer session is "How do I work with (or handle) a bad boss/employee/ subordinate?"

You can sense it REALLY bothers the questioner, but the setting and time constraints usually limit my response to a few bromides that leave neither me nor the questioner satisfied. So let me try it now at 36,000 feet in seat 12B and see what I come up with.

First, it's important to define "bad". If it's illegal, unethical, immoral or unsafe behavior then it has to be addressed and elevated to management. Otherwise you become an accomplice.

So, let's assume that we are not addressing that behavior, rather we are dealing with folks who are difficult to work with and/or uncomfortable to be around. They are a "pain".

It's a fact of life that not everyone can get along with everyone, however, I have observed that some folks "get along" better than others and I have seen them exhibit a few skills that are worth sharing.

- They put themselves in someone else's shoes before they respond. Put another way, they don't make it all about themselves. They really take the "pains" point of view and look at their world from where they are sitting. This new perspective often (not always) aids in rectifying the perceived negative behavior. (For example: "I didn't realize how overwhelmed Judy feels, we didn't give her a full orientation; we just threw her in the deep end. No wonder she is so snappy and short with folks"). After reflecting you may or may not choose to share this perspective you have with the other party.

- When they address it with the other party they pick a time and place that is unemotional. They don't address it when they are upset and/or are in a public setting where it becomes a win vs. lose event and the audience gets to pick sides. I have observed that they schedule an appointment with the other party and they have a fact-based discussion "Here's what I am observing", "what am I missing?", "can you help me clear this up?" are examples of the tone I observe.

- They listen, really listen. They come to the interaction

waiting to listen vs. waiting to talk and are patient to the extreme. It requires a suspension of their agenda and they do it to learn something instead of trying to win an argument and attack the other party.

- They offer themselves up by making it about themselves and not the other party. They come to the interaction with a "can you help me?" perspective instead of a "what's wrong with you?" attitude. That has the effect of lowering shields and engaging the other party in a helpful conversation intended to help you.

These 4 techniques can be helpful but not a panacea. There is a reason that divorce rates are so high. Some folks will be too difficult to deal with. In that case if it's a boss, you'll need to do a business case analysis to see how bad it is and if it's really that bad, develop your exit strategy. If it's a subordinate employee, you'll likewise do an analysis that ultimately analyzes their value added to the firm vs the negative behavior. As my Dad used to say about cooks in his restaurant "Is that great steak they make worth putting up with this other stuff?" Sometimes it was. Often it wasn't.

Then you have to take the view that the negative performer is taking up someone's dream job and you need to go find that dreamer.

As a leader, it may help to remember that when you have all the facts in front of you, you don't have a problem to solve. You have a decision to make.

True Growth Takeaway: Prior to "solving" a conflict, seek first to understand the other person's perspective.

True Growth Reflection: What one behavior can you improve to better resolve conflict in your professional life?

Recommended Reading: *Winning With Difficult People* by Arthur Bell and Dayle Smith

The authors point out twelve difficult personality types that can be found in business environments, then offer tips to help readers understand what makes them tick and how the rest of us can best cope with them. Advice includes methods for transforming potential problems into "getting-ahead" advantages.

CHAPTER THIRTY-TWO

"Sam, You Made the Pants Too Short!"

BOB DARE • *May 2014*

> "Oh it is great to have a Giant's strength, but it is tyrannous to use it like a Giant." —*Shakespeare (Measure for Measure)*

SERVING AS A DRILL SERGEANT was one of the most rewarding opportunities that I experienced in my 28 year Army career. It is one of the few jobs that allow you to see your leadership and training efforts evolve over 6-8 weeks, taking a raw recruit at the beginning, and marching a Soldier off of the parade field at the end.

In 1975, I was a very young Drill Sergeant with behaviors that seemed to serve me well. Entering my third cycle I was introduced to Sergeant First Class Charlie Mack who was now my immediate supervisor. Charlie was 6 foot, 3 inches, 225 pounds and extremely fit. His physical presence alone seemed to control any setting. I never heard Charlie raise his voice in anger or frustration and I noticed that he allowed trainees to carry on a conversation with him. I concluded that each leader did things in his own way and although I did not agree with Charlie's methods, he was too big to argue with.

We had a trainee, last name Rameriz. In those days soldiers were required to "blouse" their trousers inside their boots. The method we taught was quite simple: grasp your lower trouser by the inside and outside seam; place the material smoothly inside your boot; pull back on the trouser to ensure it is secure; lace your boots, tie, and tuck the laces inside the top portion of your boots; adjust the blouse so that the lower trouser portion falls evenly between the second and third eyelet of the boot.

We were in day two of the very first week of training and every time I saw Ramirez his trousers were un- bloused. This resulted in him receiving a series of verbal lashings filled with expletives and threats, followed by the command to "drop and give me ten!" (Push-ups) Each time I would correct Ramirez, he attempted to engage me in conversation. I had no desire to hear any lame excuses and besides, I was inculcating the importance of attention to detail, proper wear of the Army uniform and discipline.

Around 5:30 in the morning of day three or four, Charlie came into the mess hall (now called dining facility) and interrupted my cup of coffee. "Dare, said he, I want you to go to the barracks, call Ramirez into the office and listen to him. Do not say anything to him, do not correct his appearance, and do not have him perform push-ups or anything else until you hear what he has to say". "Yes, Sergeant", I replied somewhat snippety as I departed accordingly.

"Ramirez" I shouted as I entered the barracks, "Report to the office!" Ramirez was there almost immediately at which time I asked with authority, "Do you have something to tell me?"

"Yes, Drill Sergeant, I have been trying to tell you that these pants are too short. I have looked at the other guy's pants and their pant legs are longer. They don't have any trouble blousing their pants but no matter how hard I try my pant legs will not stay in my boot."

Wham! The proverbial two by four hit me right between the eyes as a visual inspection validated Ramirez's findings. "Go get all of your trousers and get back here ASAP", I ordered. I took Ramirez to the supply room and had our Supply Sergeant complete a turn in and reissue documents. I put Ramirez in my car and drove him to the central issue facility and 30 minutes later he was beaming from head to toe. Ramirez never said a word about my pre-reissue behavior. He constantly thanked me for resolving his dilemma.

Charlie Mack had taught me a lesson that I never forgot. From that day, whenever anyone asked to speak to me, I listened and do so today. Sometimes the message was not as important as Ramirez's was but how would I know if I did not listen?

True Growth Takeaway: Authentic leaders ask the right questions.

True Growth Reflection: What one behavior do you need to change to improve your listening skills?

Recommended Reading: *Quiet—The Power of Introverts in a World That Can't Stop Talking* by Susan Cain

The following endorsement speaks to the worth of this book: "A smart, lively book about the value of silence and solitude that makes you want to shout from the rooftops."—Daniel Gilbert, author of Stumbling on Happiness. This book will make introverts proud and challenge extroverts to speak less and learn more.

CHAPTER THIRTY-THREE

What Is Truth?

BOB DARE • *October 2016*

I AM NO SCHOLAR by any measure but I enjoy learning. The college course that I learned the most from was Philosophy. The professor who taught it made "truth" the nucleus of the course. The first question he asked was, "Where do you get your truth?" Needless to say, any work that you were required to produce for him had to clearly show that you did not restrict your efforts in research, and that you objectively presented both sides of the topic. Often, my preconceived opinion was altered, or completely changed as I gave fair consideration to an argument. Philosophy changed my process of arriving at the "truth" and although I am human, and on occasions jump to a conclusion, I am able to take a second look and alter my view as facts and information are revealed.

Of course, the opposite of truth is untruth of which there are many examples. I have found labeling to be one. Have you ever found yourself succumbing to "labeling"? We live in a world where labeling seems to be a consistent method of neatly categorizing anything including human beings. I have no idea where the concept originated. I understand the need to scientifically group species and things but I am always bothered when we attempt to define people by a label because it seems to me that labeling people is often premature and untruthful.

Consider as an example, generational labeling. I am a Baby Boomer. The label of Baby Boomer included drug user, disrespectful of law and authority, and rejecter of tradition and values, just to name a few. My son and daughter are Generation Xers. The labelers said, amongst many things, that they were antisocial, adrift, loners and anti all things organized. Each generation has been titled with a label and in many cases the label contains more negative inference than positive.

Labels, by their very design, divide. I can live with plants and foliage, mammals, reptiles, etc lumped under a category. Humans on the other hand do not need such "scientific" assessing.

Look around today and see the divisiveness that plagues us. You must be liberal or conservative; left or right; for or against whatever may be the issue of the day, and on and on and on. Many of us allow ourselves to fall prey to the "talk of the town". We ignore objectivity and critical thinking, and accept the "truth" from the "experts" and pundits who are very quick to tell us how to think. Civil debate is almost extinct; we have replaced it with arguing and shouting matches laced with profane or derogatory adjectives, non-factual claims and exaggerations that accomplish nothing but to extend the chasm between the sides. We deny ourselves the time to hear the other side because the other side does not fit our preconceived beliefs. We lump those who "are not like us" into overarching categories that normally are defined by the things we oppose and object when often, we have not taken the time to even consider a differing point of view or additional facts that may mitigate our biases.

That takes me back to my example of generational labeling. My Grandson is a Millennial (or, if you like, Generation Y). His label defines him as being all about "me", entitlement driven, lacking social skills, and so on. I recently had the opportunity to move him to college. As we approached the entry gate the road was full of young people, wearing a very friendly smile, and a colorful t-shirt with "welcome to . . . .." embossed on it. At every checkpoint along the way one of these cordial people provided direction and information until you arrived at the assigned dorm, at which time a horde of these same people descended on your automobile, asked, "What's your room number?" and, in seconds, emptied the car of its contents and delivered all of it to the room. A committee consistently passed by each dorm room offering assistance and answering questions. The atmosphere was alive with interaction, genuine concern and interest. I engaged a number of these, "me", "antisocial", young people, and through discussion found that they were all freshman students who had volunteered to assist, arrived a week early for training, were focused on the future, had great goals and expectations, were optimistic and determined to grow and ultimately contribute to our society. Not typical, you may say. Maybe so, but I am convinced that this was not the only college in this country that was enrolling young people of the ilk of my Grandson and his new classmates.

Seems to me that we need to label less, and instead, talk more, ask more, read more, and think more for ourselves if we are to ever know the "truth" about anything. Why allow a shallow, partial or biased opinion, regardless of how well it is pleasantly packaged or dynamically delivered, pull us to one side or another? We were each born with an incredible gift to think, to choose and to evaluate independent of others. Objectivity is paramount to finding the "truth".

Do yourself a favor, the next time you are being told the "truth" take some time to evaluate it, dig a little deeper into the facts, ask a few questions and then decide if that "truth" is your "truth".

True Growth Takeaway: Be careful who you allow to define your truths.

True Growth Reflection: What can I do to ensure that I am being objective when searching for truth?

Recommended Reading: *On Truth* by Harry G Frankfurt

An international bestseller with over five million copies in print, with the same leavening wit and commonsense wisdom that animates his path-breaking work *On Bullshit*, Frankfurt encourages us to take another look at the truth: there may be something there that is perhaps too plain to notice but for which we have a mostly unacknowledged yet deep-seated passion. His book will have sentient beings across America asking, "The truth-why didn't I think of that?"

CHAPTER THIRTY-FOUR

That Little Boy

Byrd Baggett • *July 2016*

> "How far you go in life depends on your being tender with
> the young, compassionate with the aged, sympathetic with the
> striving and tolerant of the weak and strong. Because some-
> day in your life you will have been all of these."
> —*George Washington Carver*

THAT LITTLE BOY WAS BORN with a smile on his face and love in his heart. That little boy loved to sing and dance. Joy always radiated from that little boy's spirit. That little boy was the third miracle to his parents, as they were told that they would never have children. That little boy had beautiful childhood relationships with his two big sisters. They sang and danced together—pure joy! That little boy loved people, no matter their color or class. That little boy had the most special bond with his mother—pure love!

That little boy thrived in elementary school and was warmly accepted by his classmates because of his gentle and loving personality. That little boy was a natural performer in school plays—you could feel the gift when he would sing and dance.

That little boy graduated into middle school and his joy soon disappeared. That little boy was called names at school and cruel things were said about his gift of singing and dancing. That little boy wanted to be part of a team and decided to try out for the 6th grade basketball team. The other boys laughed at his lack of athletic abilities, called him names, and rejected him from the team. That little boy didn't understand the hatred and came home most days with swollen, tear-filled eyes. That little boy quit smiling and retreated into a protective shell. He quit trying, his grades suffered, and he resigned himself to the fact that he was both different and inferior to his peers.

Then something good happened. His parents transferred him to a private school where he was safe to be himself. He was accepted for who he was. All students were treated with dignity and respect and were expected to treat each other accordingly. He competed in sports and experienced the joy of being part of a true team. He participated in school plays and his gift of singing and dancing blossomed. His grades improved drastically within that first year at the private school, as the teachers focused on his strengths and helped manage his weaknesses. That little boy's smile and joy returned.

That little boy and his family moved to the South where he would finish his high school years. He was entered into a public school with his sisters. He was greeted with the same taunting and name calling that he had experienced in middle school. His parents moved him to another private school where he was safe to be himself. You can feel his heart in the touching poem that was written when he was 16 years old . . .

Truly You

> There's something out there that you must find,
> For what you know, you cannot deny.
> Freedom and hope is what you need,
> If only you could truly succeed.
> All your life you strive to be the best,
> But what you really feel no one could possibly
> suppress. And as you walk onto that stage,
> This character, not what you are, is portrayed.
> Think of what you really want to be,
> And what other people really need to see. Be yourself,
> and be your best,
> And don't care about the rest.
> Because when it's time to look back at the past,
> You want to be the true you and how you came to
> be your best.
> —*Your father, Byrd Baggett*

This new high school had an excellent fine arts program that allowed him to follow his dream. The compassion and instruction of his teachers helped take his natural gifts to another level. His singing and acting skills flourished and he won numerous awards. After graduation, that little boy was accepted into the prestigious American Musical and Dramatic Academy in New York City. His parents just returned from his Showcase Performance and are so proud of their only son.

That little boy is now a man and I am very proud of him. You see, that little boy is Bryant Austin Baggett, and I love him very much. Keep soaring son!

A story book ending? Here's the rest of the story . . .

That little boy is now 30 years old and has been battling an addiction to meth since 2007. He's been in and out of over 20 treatment facilities, has attempted suicide, and has pretty much lost his will to live.

You're probably thinking, "What changed after his graduation from the American Musical and Dramatic Academy?" Shortly before his graduation, he had the courage to announce to his family that he was homosexual. Even though it was a surprise, we did not question or judge him—we just loved him more, as we knew that his journey as a gay man would not be easy—and it hasn't been.

He was not successful in fulfilling his dream of making it big on Broadway. Defeated and disillusioned, he started smoking pot to help him deal with living in the real world, a world not "gay friendly." He has, and still does, endure the taunts, sneers, anger, silence, and general hatred of those who judge him and his lifestyle. Looking for a way to escape the pain and guilt of dealing with the reality of his life, he "progressed" to meth—a battle that he continues to fight. The reality of a meth addict is that only 17% beat the addiction. That's a pretty depressing statistic. But our faith sustains us and we still believe that God can and will work a miracle in Austin's life.

Our son's journey, despite the heartache of seeing your loved one suffer, has made us much more accepting of those labeled "unacceptable" by many people. We have learned the true meaning of the words "tough love" and "unconditional love." We have learned that ignorance can lead to people—friends and family members included—saying hateful and hurtful words in public and on social media. We have learned the importance of establishing boundaries and holding firm to them—this is a hard one, especially when your son is living on the street in winter without adequate clothes, living in his car before he sold it for drug money, living in drug houses, attempting to take his life by swallowing Clorox, the list goes on . . .

What's the lesson?

#1—Don't judge people that are different than us. This includes the homeless, the poor, the incarcerated, drug addicts, people of different religious and political affiliations, people of different color, etc.

#2—Get to know and understand people who are different than us. Once we take the time to listen compassionately to others share their stories, we might, for the first time, realize the true meaning of "There but the Grace of God go I". If you're serious about accomplishing this step, go to step #3.

#3—Meet those different than us where they live. This could be a homeless shelter, a drug recovery center, a half-way house, prison, etc. This will help you understand the reality of others' lifestyles and might soften a judging and hardened heart.

#4—Get actively involved in helping those who are less fortunate than you. I'm talking about time, talents, and money (money alone doesn't qualify). It's true that where you spend your time and money is a direct reflection of your life's priorities.

#5—Love one another! If you act on steps 1-4, you will learn that God don't make junk and Love is the answer.

And son,
I will always love you.

True Growth Takeaway: Compassionate understanding is the first step to improving personal relationships.

True Growth Reflection: What action can you take to better understand a group or person "different" than you?

Recommended Reading: *The Wounded Spirit* by Frank Peretti
In his first nonfiction work, Frank Peretti examines the pain from his past and helps us uncover the scars in our own lives. Drawing from tragic news stories like Columbine, he illustrates how ridicule and rejection can push people beyond the brink. Then, with poignant insight, he shows us the way to heal the wounded spirit that lies within us all.

CHAPTER THIRTY-FIVE

The Most Important New Year's Resolution

BYRD BAGGETT • *January 2016*

> "Compassion is the basis of all morality."
> —*Arthur Schopenhauer* (German Philosopher, 1788-1860)

IT'S STATED THAT 45% of Americans make New Year's Resolutions but only 8% keep them (think workout/weight loss programs). My resolution for 2016, one we can all keep, is to keep hope alive for others by demonstrating random acts of compassion on a daily basis. In that regard, I would like to share a story that illustrates the life-changing impact of loving others. It's a story of hope that changed my life and the lives of three young children . . .

She was born in Willits, California on May 13, 1950; given up for adoption at the age of four; placed in four foster homes; prayed every afternoon that God would provide a family that, in her words, "would want me and love me"; vividly remembers that rainy day in 1955, as she was saying her prayers while looking out the picture window of her fourth foster parent's home, when she noticed a black car approaching; a man and woman got out of the car, with the man opening the back door and helping a little boy out; the woman joined her husband while cradling an infant child in her arms; the couple approached the front door and asked to meet the little girl in the window; the foster parents welcomed the adults and two children into their home and called for the little girl; the little girl approached the man and woman; they hugged her, saying, "We love you and want you to be our daughter"; Bill and Gladys Bryant, at the age of 39 and without children, adopted a daughter and two sons on that rainy day in California.

The two boys were that little girl's brothers—two year old Larry and baby Frank—who had been separated from her and placed into foster care; when Bill and Gladys Bryant went to California to adopt the four year old girl, they were told of her two brothers and decided to adopt all three. Bill and Gladys raised a beautiful and bright daughter who became the pride of their lives. I met that little girl in 1973 while she was attending college in Atlanta; we had three dates and three months later we were married; she nurtured me through the tough years of our marriage; she brought three beautiful children into this world—Ashley, Amy and Austin—who are the loves of her life. I thank God every day that Bill and Gladys Bryant adopted that little girl in 1955. Their act of courage and compassion gave me the greatest gift of life—Jeanne—my wife, best friend and hero.

I believe the true key to happiness is being a part of something greater than self by following the example of Bill and

Gladys Bryant. My prayer for you and your family is that 2016 be a year of good health and happiness.

True Growth Takeaway: Compassion keeps hope alive—share yours!

True Growth Reflection: Who in your life is struggling physically, mentally, emotionally or spiritually? What will you do today to brighten their life?

Recommended Reading: *The Compassionate Life: Walking the Path of Kindness* by Marc Barasch

How can compassion, a trait hardwired into our nervous system and waiting to be awakened, transform our lives and the world at large? Marc Barasch provides up-to-the-minute research to timeless spiritual truths, and weaves a stirring, unforgettable story of the search for kindness in a world that clearly needs it.

CHAPTER THIRTY-SIX

What Kind of Friend Are You?

Bob Clark • *October 2015*

I LOVE MUSIC and am always touched when artists capture a human emotion that causes one to reflect on incidents in life, or life in general. James Taylor does so for me in his song (written by Carole King), "You've Got a Friend."

In our True Growth seminars, we share crucibles, traumatic events that cause change in our behavior. I have had several crucibles in my life, the most recent being the sudden loss of my wife, Karen. We were married for 42 years when she passed away unexpectedly in 2013. Taylor's words were so true: "When you're down and troubled and you need a helping hand . . ." As my kids and I dealt with extreme grief, we were comforted by calls, notes and visits from friends and family members. I can remember how much it meant to us and how comforting the gestures of kindness were. They let us know we weren't alone and how much they cared about us, and we felt very grateful for their friendship.

In the two years since that awful day, I have come to understand a few lessons, not the least of which is the importance of being a good friend. I had not been as good as some of my friends who so kindly and thoughtfully supported us. What brought this to light was a rather curious phenomenon, our tragedy seemingly and surprisingly ignored by a few friends. No card, letter, phone call ... no communication at all.

I "bumped into" a few of these friends in my hometown after my wife's passing and we shared an awkward moment. They felt guilty and I felt uncomfortable. I knew they were friends, yet wondered why we hadn't heard from them. One or two even failed to acknowledge Karen's death at these encounters, puzzling me all the more. Looking back on it, I concluded they just felt very inadequate and didn't know what to say. The contrast between their behavior and that of the proactive ones taught me a good lesson on how to be a good friend, and I have tried very hard to be just that ever since.

In thinking about all of this in the context of our True Growth experience and Army service, I concluded that being a good friend to fellow Soldiers and friends during tough times (casualties, loss or serious illness/injury of a Soldier or family member) is an important characteristic of a genuine person/leader. It doesn't take much, just a call or note or short visit. An arm around the shoulder says it all. Eloquence isn't important. Just doing/saying something is. Nine times out of ten, the person experiencing the crisis puts you at ease, and you feel so much better for having made the effort. More importantly, your friend knows the answer to James Taylor's question: "Ain't it good to know, you've got a friend?"

What kind of friend are you?

True Growth Takeaway: Being, and having, a true friend is the greatest gift we can give ourselves and others.

True Growth Reflection: How many true friends do you have? What can you do to become a true friend to others?

Recommended Reading: *Same Kind of Different as Me* by Ron Hall and Denver Moore. I'll let Barbara Bush tell you why you should purchase this book . . .

"Denver Moore and Ron Hall's story is one that moved me to tears. The friendship that forms between these two men at a time when both were in great need is an inspiration to all of us to be more compassionate to everyone we come in contact with. This is truly a wonderful book!"—*Mrs. Barbara Bush*

TRUE GROWTH REFLECTION: RESPECTS/VALUES PEOPLE

Reflect on the following behaviors that are essential to being a leader who Respects and Values People:

- The leader encourages, listens to understand and then uses the input of others when appropriate.
- The leader truly cares for others and treats them fairly with dignity and respect.
- The leader strives to minimize what he/she does that adversely impacts working relationships.
- The leader empowers others to make independent decisions within his/her intent.

If you need to work on being a leader who Respects & Values People, select the one behavior that needs the most attention and develop three actions that you will work on within the next 30-90 days to shore up this competency:

1. _____

_____

_____

2. _____

_____

_____

3. _____

_____

_____

SECTION SEVEN

KNOWS SELF

CHAPTER THIRTY-SEVEN

Personal Board of Directors

Byrd Baggett • *April 2017*

> "In everyone's life, at some time, our inner fire goes out. It is then burst into flame by an encounter with another human being. We should all be thankful for those people who rekindle the inner spirit."—*Albert Schweitzer* (1875-1965)

I AM WRITING THIS ARTICLE after one of the monthly "accountability" calls with Rob Hunt and his "Personal Board of Directors".

A little background: I met Rob in 2001 after speaking at one of his organization's annual conferences. What started as a business relationship soon developed into a deep friendship, as I found Rob to be a truly authentic person. He is a man of impeccable integrity, has passion for what he does, compassion for those he serves, and, most importantly, he is a man of great humility. In other words, he's the "Real Deal".

In 2007, I invited Rob, who was enjoying a very "successful" career in the corporate world, to attend our first True Growth Academy in Kerrville, Texas. As part of the experience, we recommended that each attendee select a few individuals—their "Personal Board of Directors"—whose main task was to hold them accountable to living their True Growth® Model. I will let Rob and his "Board Members" tell the rest of the story . . .

"After attending the inaugural True Growth® Academy, I realized that I was not happy with my professional and personal growth. I also realized that a big part of my problem was that no one was helping me achieve my goals. I attributed my lack of progress to not having a "personal trainer", someone that would push me harder and encourage me to reach my goals. I knew that without this type of direction, I would continue to struggle in making the improvements that I felt were necessary. It was obvious that I would not be able to keep my personal commitments to improve without the accountability piece.

I thought about my circle of friends and my business associates and wondered who would be the most likely to help me become a better person. The names that I arrived at came to me easily and I hoped that all of my choices would accept the challenge. The reason that I chose the group was that each one of them had traits that I wanted to emulate. In short, they were all really good people with strong ethical and moral convictions, and I envied what they had achieved and the way they seemed to be "comfortable in their own skin."

As we began to function as a group, it became obvious that all of us were very compatible and in a sense, were all looking for others to help us on our life journey. Other than me, none of the others really knew each other and had not spent any time discussing serious and life changing opportunities. Today, we really function more like a peer group and everyone is able to use the "board" for their own personal issues. It has truly become a group of close personal friends and people that enjoy being around each other. Although we are very different in some aspects, we have very many things in common and have developed into a group that shares very personal thoughts and problems. In my wildest dreams, I could not have imagined that this would have worked so well and greatly appreciate my wonderful friends for all that they have done to assist me on my journey". —ROB HUNT

Feedback from Rob's Board Members . . .

"The Board of Directors has benefited me as much as (or, perhaps, more) than Rob. The effort required of personal development is never more apparent than when we're meeting together. But the reality of being able to achieve significant personal growth has also never been more clear— The group serves as a great springboard toward personal transformation which would otherwise be nothing more than a frustrated dream". —JAMES SHAY

"The Personal Board of Directors has provided me with a unique opportunity for introspection, sharing, learning, friendship and accountability in an environment of complete trust and understanding. I would highly recommend this concept to any executive seeking to be an authentic leader both at work and at home". —DAVE MARXKORS

"Being involved on a Personal Board of Directors has been a life-changing experience. A group of people with the same values trying to be the "best version" of themselves make great role models for me. I rely on this group to hold me accountable for making positive changes in my life. I hope that my sharing and friendship also helps others on the board in a similar fashion". —DON GREENLAND

"Being part of an individual's personal board has been very rewarding. I have found it to be a mutually beneficial experience and I look forward to our monthly conference calls. We have had a handful of retreats over the years—There are few other things that I take time away from my family or work for". —GREGG BRADY

I can, without reservation, state that being a part of Rob's board has benefited me more than I ever dreamed it could. I don't believe in coincidences, as I feel they are just God's way of remaining anonymous. It's not coincidental that Rob would ask me to be one of his board members in 2007, as these five men, my "brothers from other mothers", have helped me and my family deal with a family addiction that started in 2007. The monthly phone calls and annual retreats have truly been life changing, and have helped me deal with life's inevitable challenges, the addiction issue being one of many since 2007. Things would have been much harder without these men in my life.

After reading the previous words, I hope you are inspired to create your own personal board of directors, those 3-5 "kindred spirits" whose main responsibility is to hold you accountable to living a life of significance. I can assure you that it will be the best ROI of your time, energy and money.

True Growth Takeaway: There is great value in having a Personal Board of Directors.

True Growth Reflection: Would you benefit from having a Personal Board of Directors? If so, identify the 3-5 individuals you would like to have on your board and send them an invitation.

CHAPTER THIRTY-EIGHT

Whose Ball Are You Hitting?
Which Team Are You On?

VINNY BOLES • *January 2015*

28 SEPTEMBER 2014: Well, it happened again, earlier today, for the 10th time in the last 15: The European team defeated the USA in golf's Ryder Cup competition. For the uninitiated, the Ryder Cup is a biennial competition, alternating between locations in the USA and Europe, where 12 of each group's finest golfers gather to hoist the Ryder Cup in victory after three days of intense scrutiny and competition.

No sooner had the USA come up on the short end of the score (Europe's 16½ points to our 11½ points— ties earn ½ point for each team) than the recriminations began to hit the web: USA Coach Tom Watson erred in player selection and slating of his team as to who played when (or didn't play), he didn't have the personality to connect with his team of younger players (aka the age gap), Europe's Rose and Stenson shot 10 straight birdies, Europe's Graeme McDowell stormed back from four holes behind to defeat USA's Jordan Spieth—these are just the first drafts of the postmortem that will continue until 2016, when the golfing world again gathers at Minnesota's Hazeltine National Golf Course to renew the rivalry.

While listening to the broadcast, I came across a data point that, while it may be one of many, I don't think is insignificant because I believe it holds a leadership lesson for teams far removed from the golfing enterprise.

Over the competition's three days, there are three formats over 28 matches. In fourball, each golfer (two from each side) plays his own ball for 18 holes. In singles, all 12 golfers go head to head with a golfer from the other side (mano a mano). And finally, in foursomes, teams of two golfers per side play against the other team by alternating their shots. For example, USA player #1 hits the drive off the tee, USA player #2 plays that ball wherever it lies for the next shot, and then USA player #1 hits the next shot. This pattern continues until the hole is completed and then goes on for 18 holes.

My observation and subsequent lesson comes from the foursome competition. In eight foursome matches, the USA gained only one point to Europe's seven. Europe's players played their ball, regardless of who hit it. The USA players seemed uncomfortable playing a ball they didn't own ("I didn't put it there" . . . or, "I wouldn't have put it there").

How often do you have to pick up for a teammate who may (or may not) have put the ball (aka the project, the memo, the action, the decision) exactly or even close to exactly where you would have liked it? How do you react? That weekend, the Europeans reaction 87.5% of the time (seven out of eight matches) was to play their partner's ball where and how they found it and get the victory.

Do you do that? Or do you wish you had another ball? Another partner? Another team? For the 2014 Ryder Cup, Europe's foursomes played their ball for their team. We didn't appear to get that message.

The good news is that unlike the Professional Golfer's Association (PGA) you don't have to wait two years for a trip to Hazeltine in Minnesota to act on the lesson.

True Growth Takeaway: Am I meeting my teammates where they are at and rolling up my sleeves to help, or am I wringing my hands that they are my teammates?

True Growth Reflection: What three actions would make me a better teammate? Describe one positive thing that happened to you in the last 24 hours.

Recommended Reading: *The Advantage* by Patrick Lencioni

There is a competitive advantage out there, arguably more powerful than any other. Is it superior strategy? Faster innovation? Smarter employees? No, New York Times best-selling author, Patrick Lencioni, argues that the seminal difference between successful companies and mediocre ones has little to do with what they know and how smart they are and more to do with how healthy they are. This is a must read for leaders desiring to build a happy, healthy, productive and profitable organization.

CHAPTER THIRTY-NINE

It's Nice to Have a Good Buddy

Freddy McFarren • *March 2016*

GOOD LEADERS TAKE CARE OF THEMSELVES. Many do this by rugged physical fitness programs, eating right, good sleeping habits, taking time for hobbies, professional counseling and other means. Having a Good Buddy (a close friend) can be crucial to any process. The military has all sorts of proven programs to look after one's Physical Fitness, Mental Fitness, Spiritual Fitness and Emotional Fitness. A close Buddy can help with Mental/ Emotional Fitness and maybe the other two as well.

In our daily lives, we all face trials and tribulations. The profession of arms is a dangerous business as we tend to face frequent hazards. For the past decade service members and their families have dealt with a very demanding lifestyle. Preparing for deployments, deploying, combat operations and adjusting to redeployment have placed tremendous stress on the entire Military Community.

My cohort of leaders at an early time of our careers dealt with the Vietnam War. Other than the first units to arrive in

Vietnam, replacements were provided on an individual basis. The mental preparation of service members and their families was not as well done as today. Maybe worse than the preparation was the manner soldiers were treated upon their return.

My West Point class had 30 of our classmates killed in Vietnam. About 25% of our class were wounded in that war. We were the young leaders. We were proud of our service in Vietnam but we paid a heavy price. I was an advisor to a Vietnamese Ranger Battalion. There were four of us with the 600 plus Vietnamese Rangers. My counterpart had been wounded seven times and was a very courageous leader. I greatly respected him. During my year with the Rangers we lost hundreds of those very dedicated young Vietnamese. No question the loss of my classmates, the loss of other friends and those young Vietnamese Rangers deeply touched me.

Our generation did not think much of Post Traumatic Stress, depression and anxiety, but it was there and we all dealt with it in some manner or fashion. The Army Medical Community and the Veteran's Administration did and still does a good job of taking care of veterans with serious issues. However, I strongly believe that most of us dealt with emotional issues by our interactions with our Buddies. We talked about things as we knew what we had all been through. We understood one another. We knew what we faced and were facing.

I know in my case having Buddies has been very meaningful to me. One key Buddy was a young Infantry Lieutenant with the 173rd Airborne Brigade in Vietnam. For his actions during a major battle where he was wounded, he was awarded our nation's second highest award for valor. We talk on the phone often. We don't talk about Vietnam often but other life issues we all confront. Our families are close as well. I encourage all of you to think about this matter as most of you already have strong connections with fellow soldiers and friends.

My Buddy and his infantry platoon are still in close contact. He is still their LT (Lieutenant). Over the years they have helped each other through the good times and the tough times for some of them. This serves as a good example of how military reunions are so important to many service members. Their camaraderie during some hard and difficult times has become very crucial to them. Clearly a good example of the importance of interaction with one's Buddies.

The recent review about emotional issues from the wars in Iraq and Afghanistan have highlighted the fact people from all walks of life can face similar issues our military members are facing. Having family members, friends, and fellow workers who serve as a Buddy should be beneficial to our civilian counterparts as well.

Hard charging, well-meaning leaders can at times not pay enough attention to caring for themselves. Of course, that is understandable and can be seen as admirable. Most of us have a Good Buddy we interact with frequently as we conduct our daily business. Taking just a little more time to talk about issues which are on a more serious basis could in the long run be healthy from a mental perspective. Most likely these discussions will be helpful for both of you. Good Buddies are a precious resource.

True Growth Takeaway: Mental and Emotional fitness are important and may need more attention.

True Growth Reflection: What are some issues which I should discuss with my close friends?

Recommended Reading: *The Friendship Factor: How to Get Closer to the People You Care for* by Alan Loy McGinnis

At the heart of each relationship, says McGinnis, is the friendship factor-the essential ingredient of warmth and caring. With captivating case histories and anecdotes about such famous people as George Burns, Howard Hughes, and C. S. Lewis, McGinnis shares the secret of how to love and be loved. The first edition of The Friendship Factor, published in 1979, has sold more than 350,000 copies.

CHAPTER FORTY

Being A Leader

Bob Dare • *June 2016*

I FANCY MYSELF TO BE a student of leadership. I read everything that I can on the subject. I listen to those who have showed success at leading, and as a reminder of the importance of sound leadership, I keep a JFK quote hanging near my desk, "Unless Democracy can produce able leaders, its chances for survival are slight."

Many years ago, when I was thrust into a leadership position, the US Army's definition of leadership began: "The art of influencing and directing others.............". I thought that one word, "art", was so appropriate and it had a profound effect on me. When the Army removed it from its definition I was bothered. I had grown to believe that true leaders, great leaders, those who inspire, those who create a climate in which one opts to be motivated; those who stand out in the crowd, those unique peoples, were true artists.

Often, we find people miscast in positions of leadership.

They flounder, fail and fall, and in the process, they adversely impact the lives of those they were entrusted with to lead, nurture and develop.

The words you can select to define a great leader are many. If you ask ten people to provide three traits of a leader, you are apt to get thirty different words. I offer my top three below.

Loving. If you don't love people, you will never lead them. You may, for a while, capture their attention with your charisma and charm, or control them through your use of threats and fear, or get them to conform, but without commitment. None of those things reflect love, and in time, everyone will find you out, and once discovered that there is no foundation to your role, people will rebel in their own way.

You will never see the performance for which they are capable. You will never see the enthusiasm and willingness to go the extra mile. If you do not love people, your days as a leader will be limited.

Caring. Loving begets caring. People know if you really care. You can't fool them about it. When you care, you take the time to know your people; you know their ambitions, goals, and dreams; you know their families, their hobbies, what inspires them and what irks them. When you care for your people you can quickly discern when "Joan" is unhappy or something is bothering "Richard". When you care, your people care. They will go out of their way for you, and you for them. A caring environment is healthy and exciting. Innovation, creativity and candidness abound. Open, honest and meaningful dialog is second nature. In short, caring leaders create winning teams operating in a safe and wholesome environment.

DEVELOPING. When you love people and truly care for them, developing them is a natural byproduct. What do we leave when we leave an organization? A gap? A void? Confusion and disappointment? Or do we leave a well-trained team with people who are capable to replace us and to carry on those positive habits and procedures that sum to continual success. There is nothing more important and noble for a leader to leave as a legacy than people who are capable of, and eager for, continued success and achievement. Developing is giving back and there just is nothing more rewarding in life than giving.

Loving, caring and developing others takes patience and hard work. Distractors abound; but, if you are an artist, a loving, caring leader who takes pride in the awesome responsibility of developing others, your success will be of that intrinsic value that money cannot buy. The true joy, honor and privilege of leading will be your most treasured compensation.

True Growth Takeaway: Love to lead. Care to care. Develop others.

True Growth Reflection: How can I be a better leader?

Recommended Reading: *The Leadership Secrets of Colin Powell* by Oren Harari

"Powell appears to be a natural born leader with an intuitive sense of strategy for advancement in war and politics. For those of us who are not so lucky to have such diplomacy inherently, Harari's book can teach us how to lead effectively following Powell's example."—*USA Today*

CHAPTER FORTY-ONE

A Lifetime of Learning

Lawson Magruder • *November 2014*

A COUPLE OF MONTHS AGO a very special friend of mine and "Army Brother" for the past 42 years had quite an achievement earning his PhD in Philosophy from Johns Hopkins University at the age of 64. What made this achievement even more notable is that he did not serve in academia for the vast majority of his life but spent over 37 years in the service to our Nation in the most challenging positions to include Division and Corps command. He was an infantryman in peacetime and in war. Lieutenant General (Retired) Jim Dubik was an Airborne Ranger, light infantryman who commanded US forces in Haiti, Bosnia, and Iraq. He had a reputation as a "thought leader" and extraordinary trainer, tactician and strategist throughout the military. He continues to this day writing essays that are thought provoking and receive the widest dissemination in various periodicals nationally and worldwide.

Jim's creative expression and generation of ideas on a wide variety of topics does not surprise me. I saw it coming when he was a young officer in my company of paratroopers over four decades ago and have greatly admired him through the years as he continued his thirst for knowledge and desire to continuously mature as a writer and lifetime learner. Some personal observations of Jim through the years may be instructive to those of us who want to become constant learners:

- Jim's formative years in a Catholic High School and a year in a Seminary, instilled in him a very disciplined need for daily solitude, reading and self-reflection that was rare for a young military leader. This discipline continues to this day with his best writing done before dawn in the quiet confines of his home.

- Jim has always been a voracious reader of a wide variety of books and articles. From when I first met him, he always highlighted and wrote notes in the margins of his books. His personal library has hundreds of books in it and whenever I visit, I marvel that I can pull any book from the shelf and read in it his handwritten notes from decades ago. Needless to say, he always truly read every book he acquired- not skimmed through it- and made it stick by keeping notes in the book. When he drafts an essay concerning a challenging topic faced by our Nation's leaders today, he goes no further than his own personal library and vast experience to solidify his theme and his key points. When it came time to write his dissertation titled "Waging War: Filling the Gap in Just War Theory", he merely drew upon his own experiences and his own reference library.

- Jim has always wanted to share his views and learning with others. He swung away as a writer at a very young age, having articles published in various periodicals like Newsweek and various military publications. He has always loved to share and spur constructive dialogue on the most challenging topic of the day. With the advent of blogs and on-line forums, his ideas rapidly get the widest dissemination. This has been particularly important with the challenges our Nation and the world face with the rise of radical Islamic terrorist groups.

- You would think that with Jim's intense thirst for knowledge that he never achieved work-life balance in his life, but this was not the case. He was able to balance his life between his profession, family and self. His self-discipline allowed him to focus his full energy on each element of his life. When he was reading and writing and fueling his personal value of Learning, he was fully there. The same can be said about his focus on his profession and family. When he was in his unit and with his beautiful family, he was fully there with no distractions. He truly lived the most energy efficient life of any leader I know and it all came from his self-discipline and tremendous will power.

May we all strive to want to be a constant learner like my friend Jim Dubik. May we seek to gain balance in our lives as

Jim has through self- discipline and an energy efficient approach to all our endeavors.

I hope we all agree in the words of the great golfer Ben Hogan that "true enjoyment comes from constantly learning."

True Growth Takeaway: True knowledge comes from personal experiences and constant learning through disciplined reading and study.

True Growth Reflection: Are you considered a constant learner by others? If not, what can you do right now to improve your knowledge to benefit yourself, your family and others you lead?

Recommended Reading: *Mindset—The New Psychology of Success* by Carol Dweck.

Dweck, a Stanford University psychologist, has discovered a truly groundbreaking idea-the power of our mindset. Dweck explains that it's not just our abilities and talent that bring us success, but whether we approach our goals with a fixed or growth mindset. She shows how a simple idea about the brain can create a love of learning and a resilience that is the basis of great accomplishment in every area of our lives. Another great book!

TRUE GROWTH REFLECTION: KNOWS SELF

- Reflect on the following behaviors that are essential to being a leader who Knows Self:
- The leader is knowledgeable of how he/she is perceived by colleagues.
- The leader is comfortable with who he/she is.

If you need to work on being a leader who is more self-aware, select the one behavior that needs the most attention and develop three actions that you will work on within the next 30-90 days to shore up this competency:

1. _____
_____
_____

2. _____
_____
_____

3. _____
_____
_____

CONTRIBUTORS

Lawson Magruder

Founder and President of LWM III Consulting LLC, Lawson has been coaching professionals, mentoring leaders and building highly effective teams for more than four decades. He has led soldiers in combat in Vietnam and Somalia, and commanded the Joint Readiness Training Center and Ft Polk, US Army South in Panama and the historic 10th Mountain Division. Retiring as a Lieutenant General after 32 years of service, he has served as a senior leader in business and academia, and a senior mentor for Army leaders and units. He is a member of the US Army Ranger Hall of Fame, the US Army ROTC Hall of Fame and the highest ranking graduate from Army ROTC at the University of Texas at Austin. He has been married to Gloria for over 48 years and they are blessed to have three children and four grandchildren.

Byrd Baggett

Byrd is a best-selling author and popular motivational speaker. He has been helping organizations develop authentic leaders and passionately engaged teams since 1990. His corporate experience includes sales and management careers with two Fortune 500 companies. He is a Member of LWM III Consulting LLC and the creator of the True Growth brand.

Byrd is the author of 15 best-selling books on the topics of sales, customer service, leadership and motivation. A former All-American sprinter at the University of Texas at Austin, Byrd is also a Certified Speaking Professional (CSP), the highest earned designation presented by the National Speakers Association. Jeanne is his wife and best friend and they have been blessed with three children; Ashley, Amy and Austin.

Bob Dare

Bob served 28 years in the United States Army. He held every noncommissioned officer leadership position culminating with his last three assignments as Command Sergeant Major for the 25th Infantry Division, United States Army Pacific Command and United States Army Forces Command. Since his retirement, Bob has continued leading in the corporate sector. He has been the Vice President of Global Sales for two training and simulation companies. He has been part of the True Growth team since 2011. Bob and his wife of 46 years, Karen, reside in Atlanta, GA.

Larry Cole

Larry Cole, Ph.D., created the TeamMax® methodology that measures behavior change in "real-time." His methodologies drive behavioral change and answer the question, "does classroom training result in a behavior change?" His consulting success over the past three decades is based on the philosophy that *systems drive behavior change.* His discovery of the core competencies and behaviors of high performing leaders is the basis of the True Growth 360° Assessment. This assessment has helped more than 10,000 leaders become more effective in their leadership roles. He authored the 7-Step Personal Change Process™ that systemically improves individual performance and organizational change. He has published ten books and over one hundred articles. He champions the concept that *frustration is your best friend™.*

Freddy McFarren

Freddy served in the United States Army for over 37 years retiring as a Lieutenant General. The majority of his military career was spent leading/coaching soldiers at all levels. His key assignments included commanding the Fifth US Army, the 24th Infantry Division and Fort Riley, Kansas. He was also the Commandant of Cadets at West Point. Over 12 years were spent as a paratrooper with the XVIII Airborne Corps and 82d Airborne Division. His combat experience included Vietnam, Grenada, and the First Gulf War. Freddy has been a member of the True Growth team since 2011.

Bob Clark

Bob served for over 36 years in the United States Army, retiring in 2007 as a Lieutenant General. He is a distinguished Military Graduate and Distinguished Alumnus of Texas Tech University. He holds a master's degree in Political Science from

Auburn University. He commanded the Fifth U. S. Army, the 101st Airborne Division and the 3d Brigade of the 101st in Desert Shield/Storm. He served as a rifle platoon leader in the 1st Cavalry Division in Viet Nam. Following retirement from active duty, he served as a senior mentor for Army commanders preparing for deployment to Iraq and Afghanistan, and for civil support missions in the continental United States. Bob has been a member of the True Growth team since 2014. He was recently inducted into the 2016 inaugural class of the U.S. Army ROTC National Hall of Fame. He and his wife, Susan, reside in San Antonio, Texas.

Ken Keen

Ken is the Associate Dean of Leadership Development for Emory University's Goizueta Business School. Ken served 38 years in the Army retiring as a Lieutenant General. His assignments included Commander of Joint Task Force—Haiti following the 2010 earthquake, Commander of the Military Group in Colombia, Commander of the 75th Ranger Regiment, and Battalion Command of 1st Ranger Battalion and 1st 505th PIR. His combat experience includes Just Cause in Panama and Desert Storm. Ken is a distinguished military graduate from Eastern Kentucky University and a graduate of the University of Florida's Master of Arts in Latin American Studies program. Ken is a member of the U.S. Army Ranger Hall of Fame and the U.S. Army ROTC National Hall of Fame. He has been a member of the True Growth team since 2015.

Vinny Boles

Vinny Boles resides in Huntsville, Alabama. He served in the US Army over 33 years retiring as a Major General. He held leadership positions at every rank in the Army to include 5 consecutive years of service as a Commanding General after the terrorist attacks of 11 September 2001. He culminated his service as the Army's Assistant Deputy Chief of Staff, G-4 in the Pentagon. A member of the National Speakers Association, he has presented to professional associations and companies throughout the world. He holds an MBA from Babson College and BA in History from Niagara University. He is a member of the Niagara University ROTC Hall of Fame and the US Army Ordnance Corps Hall of Fame. Vinny has been a member of the True Growth team since 2011.

Byron Bagby

Byron served in the U.S. Army for 33 years and retired as a Major General. He has spent his career leading and training Army, Joint and Multinational organizations. He has served as Commandant of Joint Forces Staff College and Chief of Staff of U.S. Army Europe. He has combat experience in Grenada and Afghanistan. He earned a Master's degree in Education from UNC-Chapel Hill and a B.A. in Economics from Westminster College. He serves on numerous boards, including the Vice Chairman of the Westminster College Board of Trustees. He is a 2011 Westminster College Lifetime Alumni Achievement Award recipient. He has earned the National Association of

Corporate Directors Governance Fellow credential. Byron has been a member of the True Growth team since 2012.

Bill Weber

Bill retired from the US Army as a Brigadier General after 32 years of service. He commanded numerous units and organizations throughout his career and is a veteran of combat operations during Desert Storm in 1991 and Operation Iraqi Freedom in 2003. He also served in operations in Lebanon, Sinai, Haiti, and Bosnia and had extensive education and experience in the Middle East. Since retiring, Bill has worked in a variety of executive level positions in the corporate sector. A 1975 graduate of Texas A&M University, he has a Master's Degree in National Security Affairs (Middle East Studies) from the Naval Postgraduate School and served as Mayor of the City of Woodway, Texas. Bill has been a member of the True Growth Team since 2014.

Anne Macdonald

Anne Macdonald served in the United States Army for over 30 years and retired as a Brigadier General. She is an Army aviator and commanded Aviation units at the battalion and brigade level. She served as Deputy Director for Operations at the National Military Command Center, The Pentagon; Deputy Commanding General for 7th Infantry Division, Fort Carson; Chief of Staff, United States Army Reserve. Her final assignment was as the Deputy Commanding General for Police Development, NATO Training Mission-Afghanistan. She served in combat during the First Gulf War and Operation Enduring Freedom. Anne was in the first class to graduate with women from the United States Military Academy in 1980. She has been a True Growth team member since 2013. Anne has been happily married to her husband, John for the past 28 years.

Shane Deverill

Shane served 33 years as an Army officer and as an Army civilian. He commanded the 10th Aviation Brigade; served as Inspector General for Army Forces Command; First Army Human Resources Director, and CEO for an aviation surveillance start-up company. He served in Operation Iraqi Freedom 1 & 2. The majority of his career was spent leading, coaching, and inspiring soldiers and civilians. He is currently the strategic planner at the Defense Forensic Science Center in Atlanta. He graduated from the United States Military Academy in 1981. He has been married to Libby for 36 years; they have two sons and one grandson. Shane has been a True Growth team member since 2013.

Bob Hall

Bob retired as the 11th Sergeant Major of the Army after 33 years of service. He held numerous leadership positions including Command Sergeant Major for the Second Infantry Division, 1st US Army, and US Central Command. Upon retirement, he continued his commitment to service with his nomination to senior mentor a US Army panel dedicated to NCO Leader and

Training Development. He also served as the co-chair for the Chief of Staff, Army Retiree Council, as Vice Chairman of the Association of the US Army NCO and Soldier Programs and is currently a member of AUSA's Council of Trustees. In 2007, he was presented The Doughboy Award for outstanding contributions to the United States Army Infantry. Bob has been a True Growth team member since 2014.

Dan Elder

Dan retired as a Command Sergeant Major with more than 35 years of service. He served in a variety of units in Germany, Bosnia-Herzegovina, Croatia and Iraq. Dan's culminating assignment was as the senior enlisted advisor of Army Material Command (AMC). Dan served on the Sergeant Major of the Army's Board of Directors and has authored three books. He is a certified leadership coach and trainer. He earned a master's degree in organizational communication from Northeastern University and a BS in business administration from Touro College. He has been married to Gloria for 32 years and they have two daughters and four grandchildren. Dan has been a member of the True Growth team since 2014.

Phil Johndrow

Philip served more than 33 years in the United States Army. He has held every noncommissioned officer leadership position culminating with his last three assignments as Command Sergeant Major of the 1st Cavalry Division, Multi-National Division Baghdad and the Combined Arms Center. Phil served 42 months in Iraq as a Squadron, Brigade and Division Command Sergeants Major. Since his retirement Phil has been the National Director for Military Relations at Trident University Internal. He serves as a Senior Mentor for the Pre-Command and Command Sergeants Major Development Program. Phil has been a True Growth team member since 2013.

TRUE GROWTH LEADER DEVELOPMENT RESOURCES

Founded in 2007 by Lieutenant General (Retired) Lawson Magruder and Byrd Baggett, True Growth® was created to assist leaders in their personal and professional growth. Their mission is to help leaders embrace the transformational power of authenticity to improve themselves and the lives they touch. Over the past decade, more than 10,000 leaders have experienced the impact of True Growth® seminars, helping them unlock their potential as authentic leaders. Their staff of seasoned professional facilitators and coaches bring you or your organization an unforgettable training experience at either the legendary Gettysburg session or at a location convenient to you.

Advantages of the True Growth Experience:

- Facilitated by seasoned practitioners.

- Real world versus academic curriculum.

- Accountability Focus: True Growth 360° Assessment based on the 25 behaviors of an authentic leader, one-on-one coaching, personal and professional action plans, follow up call from the leader's personal coach to check on the progress of their action plans.

- Our coaches—with over 900 years of combined experience are experienced practitioners from the civilian, military, academic, and athletic arenas.

- Focuses on the individual and their discovery/rediscovery of personal values critical to both personal and professional development.

- Approved vendor on the GSA (General Services Administration) Schedule.

NOTE: True Growth 360° Assessment and one-on-one coaching with follow up are included in the Gettysburg True Growth Academy; optional for the one and one and a half day portable programs.

**For additional information on how we
can best serve you and your organization, visit:**

www.truegrowthleadership.com

or contact us at info@truegrowthleadership.com.